DEAD CERTAIN

by Marcus Lloyd

JOSEF WEINBERGER PLAYS

LONDON

DEAD CERTAIN
First published in 2000
by Josef Weinberger Ltd
12-14 Mortimer Street, London, W1T 3JJ

Copyright © 1999 by Marcus Lloyd

The author asserts his moral right to be identified as the author of the work.

ISBN 0 85676 239 3

This play is protected by Copyright. According to Copyright Law, no public performance or reading of a protected play or part of that play may be given without prior authorization from Josef Weinberger Plays, as agent for the Copyright Owners.

From time to time it is necessary to restrict or even withdraw the rights of certain plays. **It is therefore essential to check with us before making a commitment to produce a play.**

NO PERFORMANCE MAY BE GIVEN WITHOUT A LICENCE

AMATEUR PRODUCTIONS
Royalties are due at least fourteen days prior to the first performance. A royalty quotation will be issued upon receipt of the following details:

Name of Licensee
Play Title
Place of Performance
Dates and Number of Performances
Audience Capacity
Ticket Prices

PROFESSIONAL PRODUCTIONS
Enquiries regarding stock and repertory rights in the United States and Canada should be addressed to Josef Weinberger Plays at the address above. All enquiries regarding professional rights (excluding stock and repertory rights in the United States and Canada) should be addressed to Casarotto Ramsay & Associates Ltd, National House, 60-66 Wardour Street, London W1V 4ND.

OVERSEAS PRODUCTIONS
Applications for productions overseas should be addressed to our local authorised agents. Further details are listed in our catalogue of plays, published every two years, or available from Josef Weinberger Plays at the address above.

CONDITIONS OF SALE
This book is sold subject to the condition that it shall not by way of trade or otherwise be resold, hired out, circulated or distributed without prior consent of the Publisher. **Reproduction of the text either in whole or part and by any means is strictly forbidden.**

Printed by Commercial Colour Press Plc, London E7

To Donald Howarth
in appreciation of his generosity and enthusiasm

DEAD CERTAIN was first presented at the Theatre Royal, Windsor (Bill Kenwright, Executive Producer) on June 22nd 1999 with the following cast:

ELIZABETH   Jenny Seagrove

MICHAEL   Steven Pinder

Directed by Mark Piper

Lighting design by Matt Drury

Costumes by Lizzie Gale

Deputy Stage Manager Lindah Balfour

The action takes place in the living room of a large Victorian house in the country.

Time: the present.

Author's note:

The description of the set that MICHAEL *reads out on pages 40, 41 and 53 should, if necessary, be amended to accommodate any desired re-arrangement of the furniture.*

Also, the description of MIKE *that* MICHAEL *reads on page 42 should be altered, if need be, so as to be a more accurate description of the actor playing* MICHAEL/MIKE *but "breathtakingly handsome" should be kept. In the first production at Windsor it was changed to: "He has light brown hair, bright blue eyes and is breathtakingly handsome."*

Finally, a note on ELIZABETH'S *age. She is a former dancer who took up teaching at the age of twenty-nine but was forced to give it up following her accident seven years ago. From a purely arithmetical point of view then, she is at least in her late thirties, but could be much older. In fact I originally imagined her as being old enough to be* MICHAEL'S *mother, ie, in her fifties. However, Jenny Seagrove showed in the first production, that the part can be played to great effect by a younger woman, and if anything,* ELIZABETH'S *final words are more arrogant and provocative coming from the mouth of a woman closer to* MICHAEL'S *age. I have therefore chosen not to specify an exact age. She is older than* MICHAEL, *but exactly how much older I leave open to choice.*

Marcus Lloyd

ACT ONE

A richly furnished room of a large Victorian house. Evening. Upstage, a door to the hall. Stage right, large windows with heavy curtains. In front of the windows, a tailor's dummy. Downstage right, a comfortable armchair. Upstage, near the door, a drinks cabinet. Upstage left, a cupboard. Downstage left, a wooden desk. Off-centre, a small table. Furniture is well spaced to allow freedom of movement for a wheelchair. The walls are decorated with framed theatrical posters and playbills. Next to the cupboard hangs an aerial photograph of Brighton and behind the armchair hangs a mirror. The shelves (up and down left) are lined with books and programmes.

MICHAEL *stands centre stage looking down at* ELIZABETH *in her electric wheelchair. He is about thirty, tall and good-looking.* ELIZABETH *is older, elegant and self-possessed. Her legs are paralysed but she has full use of both arms.*

ELIZABETH (*looking at her hands*) There's blood.

MICHAEL (*looking at his hands*) My God.

ELIZABETH Is it you or me?

MICHAEL I didn't feel anything.

ELIZABETH Are you all right?

(*She takes out a handkerchief.*)

MICHAEL My God, it's everywhere.

ELIZABETH I think it's you. Come here.

(*She takes his left hand and dabs it with the handkerchief.*)

MICHAEL Your dress, I'm sorry.

ELIZABETH Must have been the brake. Use this.

MICHAEL   Thanks.

ELIZABETH   Hold it tight.

(*Using his right hand he grips the handkerchief on to his left hand.* ELIZABETH *wheels over to the desk to get some plasters.*)

ELIZABETH   Does it hurt?

MICHAEL   No. A little.

ELIZABETH   Loosen your watch.

MICHAEL   My watch?

ELIZABETH   To ease the pressure.

MICHAEL   (*holding up his clasped hands*) Well, I can't.

ELIZABETH   No, of course you can't. Here, let me.

(ELIZABETH *unstraps his watch and slips it into the pocket of his jacket.*)

MICHAEL   I'm sorry.

ELIZABETH   Nonsense. Now let's have a look.

(MICHAEL *holds out his hand for* ELIZABETH *to examine.*)

ELIZABETH   Not squeamish I hope.

MICHAEL   (*he is*) No.

ELIZABETH   Ah ha, there we are. My goodness, so much blood for such a little scratch. You must have a strong heart.

(*She squeezes out some antiseptic cream.*)

ELIZABETH   A little bit of this.

(*She applies it.* MICHAEL *flinches.*)

ELIZABETH Cold?

MICHAEL Yes.

(ELIZABETH *prepares a plaster and applies it.*)

ELIZABETH (*hamming it up*) "Will all great Neptune's ocean wash this blood clean from my hand?"

(*She looks up and smiles.*)

ELIZABETH There. All patched up.

MICHAEL Thanks.

ELIZABETH Now, what else can I get you?

MICHAEL No, nothing. Really. This is fine. I'm sorry about your dress.

ELIZABETH I'd offer you something to eat, but . . .

MICHAEL I had a sandwich on the train.

(*She dips the handkerchief into a glass pitcher of drinking water on the drinks cabinet and uses it to wash off the excess dried blood from her hands. Then she hands it to* MICHAEL *who does likewise.*)

ELIZABETH Yes, how was your journey?

MICHAEL Fine. You don't want to know.

ELIZABETH Why not?

MICHAEL I got involved in a fight.

ELIZABETH A fight?

MICHAEL Well more of a fracas really – with some schoolgirls.

ELIZABETH   Goodness.

MICHAEL   The train was packed – must have been some sort of school trip.

ELIZABETH   What happened?

MICHAEL   No idea how it started – I'd been trying to block out the noise. But suddenly there was this commotion just down from where I was standing. Three girls on one – kicking, pulling hair, that kind of thing.

ELIZABETH   And you intervened?

MICHAEL   Well, they virtually fell on top of me.

ELIZABETH   Did you get hurt?

MICHAEL   Just a couple of kicks in the shins. Then they ran off chanting "Pervert" at me, which was kind of embarrassing.

ELIZABETH   With the whole carriage watching.

MICHAEL   Yes.

ELIZABETH   And how was the girl?

MICHAEL   (*rueful laugh*) Well, she was fine. I helped her to her feet and she looked at me and said – can you believe it?

ELIZABETH   What?

MICHAEL   "Piss off, pervert," and ran off after the others.

ELIZABETH   No! What can you do! Still, I do like a good story, don't you?

MICHAEL   I'd have preferred an empty carriage.

ELIZABETH   We spend our lives hoping that things will run smoothly but when we look back it's the things that went wrong that you remember most fondly.

MICHAEL   I'm not sure 'fond' is quite the right word.

ELIZABETH   I love it when things happen. Even the bad things. I find myself formulating it into a story even as it's happening.

MICHAEL   Yes, well, we've all done that.

ELIZABETH   Have we?

MICHAEL   It's a way of dealing with difficult circumstances. I did it on the way. I thought, "This is hell but at least I'll be able to moan about it in my diary."

ELIZABETH   Are you doing it now?

MICHAEL   (*laughs*) To be perfectly honest . . .

ELIZABETH   Yes?

MICHAEL   I suppose there's always a part of me storing everything away and reworking it for later.

ELIZABETH   As a story?

MICHAEL   Yes.

ELIZABETH   Then these are "difficult circumstances"?

MICHAEL   I didn't mean that.

ELIZABETH   So, you keep a diary?

MICHAEL   Yes.

ELIZABETH   I've never had the discipline.

MICHAEL   It's nothing to do with discipline – more to do with need.

ELIZABETH I'm jealous. It must be wonderful to be able to look back and know exactly what you did and how you felt on any given day.

MICHAEL Never too late to start.

ELIZABETH How long have you kept yours?

MICHAEL Since I was a child. My mother used to insist on a couple of lines every night. She kept hers in the front of the book and I wrote mine at the back. It became a habit. I find it very . . .

ELIZABETH Therapeutic?

MICHAEL It helps me clarify my thoughts.

ELIZABETH I'm sure it does. How will it start – today's entry?

MICHAEL That probably depends on how it ends.

ELIZABETH Maybe I will start. Tonight when you've gone, I'll write it all down, too.

MICHAEL If you're nice about me, I'll be nice about you.

ELIZABETH Deal. Because at the moment, for me it's . . . I mean, I imagine I'm telling my little story to . . .

MICHAEL Who?

ELIZABETH Richard and Judy. You know, on the telly. I imagine I'm on there having a nice cosy chat, telling stories. And they're laughing and giving me coffee. As if they'd ever have me on. And how was my map and the instructions?

MICHAEL Very clear.

ELIZABETH Good.

MICHAEL Although, come to think of it, I did have a little trouble with the . . .

ELIZABETH	It's a nuisance, isn't it?
MICHAEL	What?
ELIZABETH	The gate.
MICHAEL	(*puzzled*) Yes.
ELIZABETH	I keep meaning to get it fixed. One of these days.

(*She wheels over to the drinks cabinet.*)

ELIZABETH	Drink?
MICHAEL	How did you know?
ELIZABETH	What?
MICHAEL	That I meant the gate.
ELIZABETH	(*seriously*) Oh, I have special powers. (*Then lightening.*) Actually everyone has trouble with it. There's a knack. I should have mentioned it in my letter.

(*She holds up the decanter of Scotch as a question.*)

MICHAEL	Oh, no thanks. Water's fine.
ELIZABETH	Water? Oh I see. Of course, for your throat. I'll have some too, why not?

(*She checks the now discoloured drinking water.*)

ELIZABETH	Ah. Slight problem.
MICHAEL	Ah.
ELIZABETH	(*calling*) Estelle? (*To* MICHAEL.) Did you get it open in the end?
MICHAEL	No actually, I climbed over.

ELIZABETH Estelle! Really? You climbed over?

MICHAEL Yes. I think she may have gone out.

ELIZABETH You mean you saw her?

MICHAEL Well, I presume it was her. I arrived as she was leaving.

ELIZABETH Oh, what a bore. So now what are we going to do? Are you sure I can't tempt you with something else?

MICHAEL Well, if it makes it easier.

ELIZABETH It does rather.

MICHAEL Coke or something.

ELIZABETH Coke? Yes we've got that. Can't stand it myself but Estelle guzzles it down. Tell me, what did you think of her?

MICHAEL Estelle?

ELIZABETH Yes.

MICHAEL We hardly spoke. I came in, she went out.

ELIZABETH What did she say?

MICHAEL Well, it was strange actually. I couldn't make it out. Something about a placard.

ELIZABETH A placard?

MICHAEL "Look in the placard." I think. Didn't understand.

ELIZABETH Well, she's an odd one. French, you know.

MICHAEL Yes, I thought so.

ELIZABETH Very pretty.

MICHAEL	I couldn't tell. She had her scarf up.
ELIZABETH	Yes, of course. She's a lovely girl. And what an amazing figure!
MICHAEL	Well . . .
ELIZABETH	So voluptuous. I've always wondered what it would be like to have long legs and big breasts.

(ELIZABETH *hands* MICHAEL *his drink.*)

Cheers.

MICHAEL	Cheers. (*He takes a sip.*) Oh, you've put something in this.
ELIZABETH	Just a drop of brandy.
MICHAEL	Thank you, but I'd prefer it straight.
ELIZABETH	You don't like it?
MICHAEL	Not when I'm working. I try to make it a rule.
ELIZABETH	Oh, I don't mind.
MICHAEL	Well . . .
ELIZABETH	Please. I don't want you to think of this as work. Come on, relax. Feel at home.
MICHAEL	Well, if you insist.
ELIZABETH	Yes, I do.
MICHAEL	All right then, just the one.

(*He takes another sip.*)

ELIZABETH	Good, good. Now, I'd like to have a proper look at you, if you don't mind.

(Michael takes a pace towards her. She takes both hands and gazes at him.)

Oh yes, perfect. Perfect.

(She pulls him a little closer and he accidentally steps on her foot which has slipped off the foot-rest of the wheelchair.)

MICHAEL   Oh, I'm sorry.

ELIZABETH   What?

MICHAEL   Your foot, I'm sorry.

ELIZABETH   Was it? Is it all right?

(Michael bends down and repositions it on the foot-rest.)

ELIZABETH   Is this you getting your own back?

MICHAEL   What?

ELIZABETH   First I tread on your toes, then you tread on mine.

(She smiles.)

ELIZABETH   Can't feel a thing down there. Completely senseless. Mind you I'm not sure there's much sense up here either. If I had any sense I'd have . . . sorry, don't get morbid, Elizabeth. How clever of Mr Sacks to find you.

MICHAEL   Let's hope I can live up to your expectations.

ELIZABETH   Did he explain the financial arrangements?

MICHAEL   Yes.

ELIZABETH   And they are satisfactory?

MICHAEL   Most generous.

ELIZABETH	Estelle saw you at The Queen's Arms.
MICHAEL	Ah.
ELIZABETH	I sent her on a recce. *Two's A Crowd* or something.
MICHAEL	*Three's A Crowd*.
ELIZABETH	Yes of course. *Three's A Crowd* and two's company. I'd have gone myself but it's not very dignified being carried up all those stairs. Such a shame to have missed it.
MICHAEL	Well, it was nothing wonderful.
ELIZABETH	Oh, but Estelle loved it.
MICHAEL	Did she?
ELIZABETH	Couldn't stop talking about it.
MICHAEL	What did she say?
ELIZABETH	About you?
MICHAEL	About the whole thing.
ELIZABETH	She said you were one of the stars.
MICHAEL	There were only the three of us in it.
ELIZABETH	But even so! Apparently you had to appear without your clothes at one point. Completely starkers, Estelle said. That must have been quite a challenge.

(MICHAEL *shrugs*.)

Such a shame about those stairs.

(*She lowers her eyes and her gaze lingers on his crotch.*)

ELIZABETH   I'm sorry, I'm embarrassing you.

MICHAEL   Not at all.

ELIZABETH   By all accounts you had very little to be embarrassed about. Or do I mean a lot? I'm sorry Michael, we've only known each other two minutes and already we're talking about sex. Tell me . . . oh no, I couldn't possibly.

MICHAEL   What?

ELIZABETH   No, I . . .

MICHAEL   What?

ELIZABETH   I've always wondered about these kind of things.

MICHAEL   Yes?

ELIZABETH   Weren't you worried you might get, you know . . . without your clothes on?

MICHAEL   Aroused?

ELIZABETH   Yes.

MICHAEL   In front of so many strangers?

(*He shakes his head, no.*)

ELIZABETH   So you'd be no good in one of those films then? Tell me, would you say you were the sort of person who makes things happen or are you the type that things happen to?

MICHAEL   I would say I am the sort of person who would like to get to work.

(*He takes off his jacket and hangs it up.*)

ELIZABETH   Ah ha, that's what I like to see! Enthusiasm. You strike me as being a bit of a go-getter. Tell me, how do you feel when faced with choice?

MICHAEL   How do I feel?

ELIZABETH   Yes.

MICHAEL   (*shrugs*) I don't know.

ELIZABETH   No, please. I mean it.

MICHAEL   Well it depends. What choice are we talking about?

ELIZABETH   Just generally.

MICHAEL   (*shrugs*) I suppose I feel anxious sometimes.

ELIZABETH   Yes?

MICHAEL   Sometimes hopeful.

ELIZABETH   What else?

MICHAEL   If I'm honest . . .

ELIZABETH   Yes?

MICHAEL   Sometimes I feel a sense of inevitability.

ELIZABETH   Inevitability?

MICHAEL   Sometimes.

ELIZABETH   Why?

MICHAEL   All these questions.

ELIZABETH   I'm a nosey parker, aren't I? Well?

MICHAEL   What?

ELIZABETH   Why do you feel a sense of inevitability?

MICHAEL   I don't know. Sometimes in certain situations I just get a feeling that I'm not actually choosing, I'm just responding according to who I am – you know, my genes, chemistry, whatever.

ELIZABETH You've been pre-programmed?

MICHAEL Maybe.

ELIZABETH How fascinating. And what else do you feel?

MICHAEL Well, nothing.

ELIZABETH At all?

MICHAEL Why, what do you feel?

ELIZABETH Power, Michael. Power. At least I used to. I'm sure you make things happen all the time. I admire that. It's terribly frustrating sitting around waiting. I do miss the theatre! There was a time when I'd seen everything in the West End. Every night I'd go up on the train. I had to ration myself. I ended up seeing some things twice . . . three or four times even. It's not that I can't discriminate. I know what I like. It's just that I like the things I don't like too. If you see what I mean.

MICHAEL Not exactly.

ELIZABETH Some things inspire me because they are good, others because well, frankly, I feel I could do better myself.

MICHAEL So you've decided to have a go.

ELIZABETH Oh Michael, you make me sound like some sort of crank. I'm not some eccentric cripple having a bash because she's got nothing better to do.

MICHAEL Of course not.

ELIZABETH I've been doing classes. This is important to me.

MICHAEL Yes, I can see . . .

ELIZABETH   I expect full co-operation.

MICHAEL   Of course.

ELIZABETH   Four hundred pounds is a lot of money.

(*She wheels over to the desk and opens the drawer.*)

I haven't got much in the way of props.

(*She takes out two revolvers.*)

But I thought these would help bring it to life a bit. Go on, take one.

(MICHAEL *takes one and weighs it in his hand.* ELIZABETH *points her gun at him.*)

ELIZABETH   Apparently, the rule is: introduce them early on. I've been reading about it. Validate their existence early on so that when they're used later there is no danger of it all seeming too easy or contrived.

MICHAEL   And you've done that in yours?

ELIZABETH   Oh yes. I mean guns don't just appear from nowhere.

(ELIZABETH *points her gun at him.*)

ELIZABETH   Now point it at me and move over. Just a bit. That's it. (*Suddenly angry.*) I said point it at me!

(MICHAEL *obeys, suddenly a little frightened.*)

ELIZABETH   Go on, finish me off. Finish what you started all those years ago. I said shoot, damn you. Life or death, Michael? Five. Four. Three . . .

MICHAEL   Hold it.

ELIZABETH   Two . . .

MICHAEL   Wh-what do you . . . ?

ELIZABETH   One . . .

(On the next beat she pulls the trigger. But there's no bullet, just a click.)

MICHAEL   Jesus.

ELIZABETH   Excellent. Excellent. Of course in actual fact it would be he who fires. Are you all right? I didn't mean to . . .

MICHAEL   *(weighing the gun)* No, no it's just . . .

ELIZABETH   Realistic, aren't they? Estelle's a wonder. She says their easier to get hold of than you'd imagine.

(She takes the gun from him and puts them both back in the drawer.)

ELIZABETH   I'll keep them safe 'til we need them. I had toyed with other ideas – strangulation, poison, electrocution, that sort of thing. But there's something very satisfying about guns, isn't there? It's so instant. You're alive, alive, alive, bang, dead. Assuming you do it right of course.

(She picks up two bound, typewritten scripts from a shelf. She hands one to MICHAEL.*)*

There you go. They've come out quite nicely, all printed up and bound.

(She keeps one for herself and flicks through it.)

ELIZABETH   Now, let's see. What shall we do first? I'm tempted to jump in at the deep end. There's a particular scene . . .

MICHAEL   Whatever.

ELIZABETH   But it's a bit, well, you know.

MICHAEL What?

ELIZABETH Risqué.

MICHAEL Ah.

ELIZABETH But it might break the ice.

MICHAEL Assuming the deep end is still frozen.

ELIZABETH Let's do it.

(MICHAEL *sits down in the armchair.*)

MICHAEL Perhaps you could give me a little bit of background first.

ELIZABETH Such as?

MICHAEL Who am I? Where do I come from? Where am I going? That sort of thing.

ELIZABETH I'm sure you are better qualified to answer those questions.

MICHAEL But you are the author.

ELIZABETH When you say, "Where do I come from?" do you mean geographically?

MICHAEL No I mean background, and . . .

ELIZABETH Parents?

MICHAEL Yes, in part.

ELIZABETH But I haven't given it any thought.

MICHAEL Well, you must. You should be able to write a full biography of all your characters.

ELIZABETH (*thinks*) Parents, parents. Who were *your* parents?

MICHAEL	You can't do it like that. My parents are *my* parents. Not the character's.
ELIZABETH	Your mother was a housewife and your father was a musician.
MICHAEL	OK, what sort of musician?
ELIZABETH	No, I'm guessing. Am I close?
MICHAEL	I don't think it's relevant.
ELIZABETH	But it's interesting.
MICHAEL	My mother was a . . . she worked in cabaret.
ELIZABETH	Doing what?
MICHAEL	She was in a troupe called the Bluebells. They were . . .
ELIZABETH	I know who the Bluebells were. Of course I do. Showgirls. Very leggy. Topless.
MICHAEL	Yes.
ELIZABETH	How thrilling. And your father?
MICHAEL	I'm told he was a civil servant.
ELIZABETH	He died?
MICHAEL	No. I did track him down once but he didn't want to know.
ELIZABETH	Bastard! Him, I mean, not you. So your mother brought you up on her own.
MICHAEL	She gave up her career.
ELIZABETH	You must be very close.

(MICHAEL *shrugs*.)

ELIZABETH	Well, this is all far more interesting. Can I steal it?
MICHAEL	For the character?
ELIZABETH	Yes.
MICHAEL	I don't think I've made myself clear, have I? Why don't you just tell me what you *do* know about the character.
ELIZABETH	Well, mmm, oh gosh . . . he's made up of opposites. He's fond of adventure but he likes security. He's ambitious but fatalistic. He's . . . what's the word?
MICHAEL	Confused?
ELIZABETH	No. Oxymoron. He's oxymoronic. Which sounds worse than it is. He's made up of opposites and contradictions.
MICHAEL	OK.
ELIZABETH	He's the sort of person who would be confident enough to, well, stand naked on stage, but his self-belief is fragile.
MICHAEL	OK. And what does he do?
ELIZABETH	In the play?
MICHAEL	I mean what's his job, his profession?
ELIZABETH	Acting.
MICHAEL	Oh, he's an actor?
ELIZABETH	Yes.
MICHAEL	So then it's about what?
ELIZABETH	Do you mean its plot or its theme?
MICHAEL	Both.

(She wheels over to the bookshelf and selects a book.)

ELIZABETH My teacher gave me this. Do you know it?

(He takes it from her and reads the title.)

MICHAEL *The Right to Write.* No.

(She takes it back.)

ELIZABETH He calls it the Bible. It's got everything we need to know. Here we are. "It is important to distinguish between theme and plot. The theme is what the play is about. The plot is the vehicle used to convey the theme or themes." Now, I've written mine down somewhere. Ah yes, here we are: Freedom, empowerment, identity.

MICHAEL Freedom, empowerment, identity.

ELIZABETH You don't like them?

MICHAEL On the contrary, they sound most interesting.

ELIZABETH I do hope so. As to plot, well I'd rather not spoil it.

MICHAEL Remember that I'm an actor, not an audience. If I am going to do justice to your work you are going to have to let me in on your secrets.

ELIZABETH I suppose I could just tell you how it begins.

MICHAEL OK.

ELIZABETH It starts off when you arrive at the private house of a crippled woman to read a play she has written.

MICHAEL You're joking.

ELIZABETH Not at all.

MICHAEL   The play is about an actor who comes to read a play?

ELIZABETH   Yes.

MICHAEL   What's that play about?

ELIZABETH   Nothing. It's just a pretext.

MICHAEL   For what?

ELIZABETH   To get him there.

MICHAEL   Why?

ELIZABETH   I don't want to spoil it.

MICHAEL   (*laughs*) It sounds . . .

ELIZABETH   Intriguing?

MICHAEL   Complicated.

ELIZABETH   Not at all. (*Referring to her book.*) "Write what you know. That which you do not know you must research. Remember your own experience of life is unique."

MICHAEL   No prizes for guessing who you're playing.

ELIZABETH   Unfortunately Estelle is not interested in acting. That's what this is for. (*She points at the dummy.*) And to be honest, just between us, there's not much difference. Now, I want your honest opinion. If you don't like it you must say so. Be ruthless. I'm not proud. If a line doesn't work you must tell me.

(*She holds up a pencil.*)

ELIZABETH   And I'll make a note. Top of page twenty. Perhaps you could read the stage directions.

(MICHAEL *finds the page.*)

MICHAEL   I am Mike?

ELIZABETH   And I am Liz.

MICHAEL   Well that's easy to remember.

ELIZABETH   I'll change them later, of course.

(*He begins to read from the script.*)

MICHAEL   "Mike stands and walks towards Liz. He bends down and kisses her passionately on the lips. She makes no response. He straightens and turns to Estelle. He advances on her and comes up behind. He cups his hand under her left breast and kisses her neck. She stands unmoved."

ELIZABETH   Good. You can stop there.

(*She wheels a little closer, settles herself and waits expectantly.*)

MICHAEL   You want me to do that?

ELIZABETH   Yes.

MICHAEL   In the interest of character development don't you think we should start somewhere else?

ELIZABETH   Oh, don't be such a prude.

MICHAEL   I would need to understand why.

ELIZABETH   Because of the play, Michael. The play.

MICHAEL   But I can't just make an unprompted sexual advance.

ELIZABETH   He's prompted by the script. Liz has her motives. She hasn't written it simply for the sake of something to do. It is a means to an end.

MICHAEL   What end?

ELIZABETH	The end of her sexual frustration. Believe me, it's not easy. When you are suddenly and unexpectedly crippled you have little or no hope of a fulfilling sex life, and certainly not with a handsome young man like Mike.
MICHAEL	How do I know this isn't *your* motive?
ELIZABETH	(*laughs*) Yes I admit it's been a little problematic. But I still have friends. They didn't all just disappear because I . . . became like this. Even a cripple can enjoy sex.
MICHAEL	Remarkable how you can argue both sides to the same end.
ELIZABETH	Thank you.
MICHAEL	I'm not sure I meant it as a compliment.
ELIZABETH	Shall we proceed?
	(MICHAEL *stands, takes a deep breath and prepares himself inwardly.*)
ELIZABETH	In your own time.
	(MICHAEL *opens his eyes and walks towards* ELIZABETH. *He bends down and kisses her on the mouth.*)
ELIZABETH	(*whilst engaged in the kiss*) More passionately.
	(MICHAEL *obliges. He straightens and turns to the dummy. He advances on it and takes a pace to his right.*)
ELIZABETH	Other way.
	(MICHAEL *corrects himself and standing behind the dummy he cups his hand under the left breast and kisses its neck.*)

ELIZABETH (*applauding*) Bravo. How was it for you?

(MICHAEL *gestures that he doesn't know what to say.*)

ELIZABETH I must say I rather enjoyed it. (*To the dummy.*) He's not a bad kisser, is he? Not bad at all. I've never kissed anyone for the sake of art before. I've always wondered what it was like, you know, kissing someone on the stage when you're only just getting to know them in real life.

MICHAEL And now you know.

ELIZABETH Like Burton and Taylor, Olivier and Leigh. Did you think it worked?

MICHAEL It's not for me to say.

ELIZABETH But did it have dramatic tension?

MICHAEL It's out of context.

ELIZABETH Let's run through it once again.

MICHAEL D'you know, I think it would be better for both of us if we started at the beginning?

ELIZABETH That's something my teacher's always saying.

MICHAEL What?

ELIZABETH That people seldom say what they really mean.

MICHAEL Which means?

ELIZABETH Which means, I think you are trying to say that you feel uncomfortable and embarrassed about kissing me.

MICHAEL It's just that I don't feel I can give you my best unless I know more background.

ELIZABETH   And so the game continues. Surely you've had a stage kiss before?

MICHAEL   No.

ELIZABETH   Oh, come on. You've appeared naked but you've never kissed anyone. What about *West Side Story*?

MICHAEL   That was different.

ELIZABETH   Mr Sacks told me you had a kiss in that.

MICHAEL   He had no business to.

ELIZABETH   He's your agent.

MICHAEL   And I am an actor. Not some sort of . . .

ELIZABETH   You mean there's a difference.

MICHAEL   Of course there's a difference.

ELIZABETH   Between what?

MICHAEL   Acting and what you are insinuating.

ELIZABETH   And what am I insinuating?

MICHAEL   I am not here as some sort of male escort.

ELIZABETH   They say prostitutes will never kiss a stranger. But actors do it all the time don't they?

MICHAEL   Now listen. I didn't come here to be insulted.

ELIZABETH   Of course you didn't.

MICHAEL   Either we do this properly or what's the point?

ELIZABETH   Yes, of course.

(*Pause.* MICHAEL *attempts to remain stern-faced.*)

ELIZABETH   Forgive me?

(*She looks at him impishly. He smiles despite himself.*)

You're going to have to keep me in my place. You actors have always fascinated me and I so rarely get to speak to any these days.

MICHAEL   Why don't we go over some lines?

ELIZABETH   They say acting isn't just about the words that are spoken.

MICHAEL   Well, yes, but you've got to give me something to work with.

ELIZABETH   I'm not sure you'll be impressed by my dialogue.

MICHAEL   Shall we try?

ELIZABETH   At the moment I'm more concerned about the plot – getting the characters to do what I want them to do. Like with the guns, I know what has to happen, but the actual mechanics . . .

MICHAEL   OK, well let's work on that. If you want me to improvise then that's fine.

ELIZABETH   You don't mind?

MICHAEL   (*with enthusiasm*) No.

(*He takes the guns from the drawer and hands one to her.*)

So give it to me again. She wants him to shoot her. Is that right?

ELIZABETH   In the end, yes.

MICHAEL   OK, good. So that's where we're heading. Now why does she want him to shoot her?

ELIZABETH	Because she's lost the will to live. And because she's found a reason to die.
MICHAEL	Which is?
ELIZABETH	To cause him pain.
MICHAEL	In what way?
ELIZABETH	Have you ever killed anyone?
MICHAEL	No.
ELIZABETH	Can you imagine killing anyone?
MICHAEL	Yes, I think so.
ELIZABETH	Really? You think you are capable?
MICHAEL	Given certain circumstances.
ELIZABETH	Such as?
MICHAEL	If I saw a man spraying bullets at school children and I had a gun.
ELIZABETH	And how would you feel afterwards?
MICHAEL	Well terrible – shaken up, I imagine.
ELIZABETH	You'd have nightmares.
MICHAEL	Probably.
ELIZABETH	And you'd think about it every day for the rest of your life.
MICHAEL	Quite possibly. Yes.
ELIZABETH	Well then.
MICHAEL	It's a punishment. The horror of killing someone.
ELIZABETH	Exactly.

MICHAEL   Punishment for what?

ELIZABETH   Because he's responsible.

MICHAEL   For her condition?

ELIZABETH   Exactly.

MICHAEL   How?

ELIZABETH   He was negligent and irresponsible.

MICHAEL   But he doesn't want to shoot?

ELIZABETH   No, of course not.

MICHAEL   Why not?

ELIZABETH   Would you?

MICHAEL   I don't know.

ELIZABETH   You're not a cowboy or a gangster.

MICHAEL   I'm an actor.

ELIZABETH   Exactly. Never held a gun before in your life. Not a real one at any rate. It's a case of two birds with one stone. She wants to die and she wants him to suffer. Either he kills her and gets a life time of guilt and quite probably life in prison for murder or she kills him and then kills herself. Life or death, you see. I must say life has always seemed to me to be the greater punishment.

MICHAEL   But he wouldn't get life would he? Not if he argued self-defence.

ELIZABETH   Against a frail cripple?

MICHAEL   If he explained the circumstances.

ELIZABETH   To whom?

MICHAEL	I don't know . . . the police, whoever.
ELIZABETH	So that?
MICHAEL	So that he'd be let off. Wouldn't he? Unless there's something I don't know.
ELIZABETH	No, you're right. And that's how I want it. I want him to shoot. So that must be his best option.
MICHAEL	OK, let's try it and see if it works.
ELIZABETH	OK.

(*They point the guns at each other.*)

MICHAEL	OK.

(MICHAEL *assesses the situation. He sees a snag.*)

MICHAEL	Ah, no, you see.
ELIZABETH	What?
MICHAEL	Already . . . don't you see? If I shoot it doesn't mean you have to die. If I was really in this situation I'd shoot you in the arm. Then I'd overpower you.
ELIZABETH	Would you?
MICHAEL	So neither of us die.
ELIZABETH	Yes, of course.
MICHAEL	If you're forcing him to shoot you, it's not so easy. You're saying he has only two options but I can see others.
ELIZABETH	But I must have it that if he shoots she dies.
MICHAEL	In that case . . .

(*They ponder.*)

ELIZABETH　How about if she disabled him first?

MICHAEL　How?

ELIZABETH　Shooting him in the leg.

MICHAEL　Mm.

ELIZABETH　Before she gives him the gun.

MICHAEL　It's not his gun?

ELIZABETH　No.

MICHAEL　OK. Let's try it.

(*He hands back the gun.*)

MICHAEL　So I'm standing here unarmed. Let's get it clear. You want to force me to shoot you. I want to get out of this situation. Right, OK. Conflicting desires, that's good. So you're aiming at my legs, threatening to disable me. What would I do? I could run for the door.

(*He runs to the door.*)

ELIZABETH　But I'd shoot.

MICHAEL　Right. Or I could . . . (*He hides behind the dummy.*) . . . use this as protection.

ELIZABETH　Not much protection. I can still see your legs.

MICHAEL　Or I could go here.

(*He stands behind the armchair.*)

ELIZABETH　I'd still get you eventually.

(*He ponders.*)

MICHAEL   How about if . . .

(He edges closer along the line of fire.)

. . . I edge closer. We lock eyes.

(They lock eyes.)

I'm psyching you out. Then . . .

(With a sudden movement he grabs at the gun. ELIZABETH is too quick and holds it out of reach. They look at each other and then both shake their heads.)

ELIZABETH   I'd still shoot.

MICHAEL   Yes.

ELIZABETH   So. *(Aiming at his legs.)* Bang.

MICHAEL   And I fall to the floor in agony.

(He lies down on the floor.)

ELIZABETH   Yes, and I wheel closer.

MICHAEL   Yes.

(She wheels closer.)

ELIZABETH   And hand you the other gun. Very slowly. Keeping this other one trained on you all the time.

MICHAEL   Yes.

ELIZABETH   You reach for the gun.

(He reaches for the gun.)

MICHAEL   But you're still worried I might pull a fast one.

ELIZABETH   Yes. So . . .

MICHAEL   Another shot?

ELIZABETH   Why not?

MICHAEL   To my other leg this time.

ELIZABETH   Bang.

            (MICHAEL *mimics agony.*)

ELIZABETH   I hand you the gun.

MICHAEL   And by now I'll do anything you want because the pain is unbearable and a third shot would be too much.

            (MICHAEL *reaches for the gun.*)

ELIZABETH   (*improvising*) "Slowly, slowly. Keep it pointed at my head."

MICHAEL   Yes, good. Of course, it's hard for me.

ELIZABETH   Why?

MICHAEL   Because I'm in agony.

ELIZABETH   I keep this one pointed at you. You'd be trembling, I think.

MICHAEL   OK.

            (*He starts to tremble.*)

MICHAEL   What now? The countdown?

ELIZABETH   Actually, I've got a little speech.

MICHAEL   OK.

ELIZABETH   But I'll save it for later.

MICHAEL   So then you count down.

ELIZABETH   (*fast*) Five four three two one.

MICHAEL   And I have no option but to . . . bang.

ELIZABETH   Yes. I slump backwards. Dead. Victorious. Free at last.

(*She savours the moment.*)

MICHAEL   And I look on in horror at what I've done – the blood and the brains. Elizabeth? Are you OK?

ELIZABETH   Sorry. Got caught up. What did you say?

MICHAEL   That I'd be looking on at the blood and brains, horrified.

ELIZABETH   Yes. We'd have to have a special effect.

MICHAEL   An image that will haunt me.

ELIZABETH   Yes. For life.

MICHAEL   What then? Curtain?

ELIZABETH   Yes.

(MICHAEL *stands up.*)

MICHAEL   How's that?

ELIZABETH   Oh, I like it! Yes, much, much better. You know, I saw it once in a play. Can't remember which one. Young man sits down, puts a gun in his mouth, pulls the trigger – brains and blood spatter on the wall behind. Very effective. Of course it must have come out of the back of the chair.

MICHAEL   But do you see the point – you don't want people saying "Why didn't he do this or that?"

(ELIZABETH *takes the gun from* MICHAEL *and puts both guns back in the drawer.*)

ELIZABETH Oh yes, yes . . . and if you looked carefully at the set before it happened, as I did, you could see faint blood stains on the walls from the previous performances. I can't tell you how exciting it is – making it real. It's all very well trying to use your imagination but it's not until you actually do it, is it, that you can see if it'll work. You're a very talented young man.

MICHAEL It's basic technique.

ELIZABETH And modest. We still haven't done any dialogue.

MICHAEL There is one thing, though.

ELIZABETH What?

MICHAEL If it was me, I wouldn't pull the trigger.

ELIZABETH You wouldn't?

MICHAEL Not if I was really in that situation.

ELIZABETH That's very brave.

MICHAEL It's nothing to do with bravery. It's just . . . well, I just don't think I could do it.

ELIZABETH You'd rather die?

MICHAEL I don't think I could kill someone.

ELIZABETH So then you're saying that it won't work.

MICHAEL I'm saying that I'd have to find a part of myself that would pull the trigger.

ELIZABETH Perhaps that'll happen as we progress.

MICHAEL Why don't we start at the beginning?

ELIZABETH Tell me more about *West Side Story*.

MICHAEL There isn't much to say.

ELIZABETH   It's one of my favourites. (*Singing*.) "Tonight, tonight . . ." You know I must have seen it twenty times over the years. Who were you?

MICHAEL   You mean my agent didn't tell you?

ELIZABETH   He said he shouldn't have mentioned it.

MICHAEL   I was in the chorus.

ELIZABETH   It's a big show to do on the fringe.

MICHAEL   It wasn't on the fringe.

ELIZABETH   Oh, but I don't understand. I'm sure I heard London. Surely you don't mean . . . not the West End?

MICHAEL   Yes.

ELIZABETH   You're joking. You're having me on.

MICHAEL   No.

ELIZABETH   When?

MICHAEL   Five or six years ago.

ELIZABETH   You're pulling my leg. You're pulling the leg of a poor old cripple. Swear to me.

MICHAEL   It's not that big a deal.

ELIZABETH   Oh, but it is! Go on. I mean it. Swear to me. (*Then humbly*.) Please.

MICHAEL   (*feeling faintly ridiculous*) I swear that I was in *West Side Story* a few years ago.

ELIZABETH   Oh, but that's wonderful. I saw it. I saw it five times. Oh . . . oh . . . Michael it was fantastic. It was one of the best things I've ever seen. But you

	know I don't remember any of the chorus having a stage kiss.
MICHAEL	It's not the sort of thing you would remember.
ELIZABETH	Oh, but I'm very keen on detail.
MICHAEL	I also understudied Tony.
ELIZABETH	You didn't! You're teasing me. Did you ever go on?
MICHAEL	It's over and forgotten about.
ELIZABETH	Oh, don't be like that. I bet you were terrific.
	(*No response.*)
ELIZABETH	Michael?
MICHAEL	I went on for one week.
ELIZABETH	That's wonderful.
MICHAEL	Stephen took an overdose.
ELIZABETH	Of drugs?
MICHAEL	It was an accident. His first time.
ELIZABETH	That's terrible.
MICHAEL	He was off for a year.
ELIZABETH	But that wasn't your fault. You grabbed your chance.
MICHAEL	Yes.
ELIZABETH	You should be proud. You don't want your agent to hide something like that.

(*She wheels over to the shelf.*)

ELIZABETH   When was it exactly?

MICHAEL   I can't remember.

ELIZABETH   I know it was ninety-two. But which month?

MICHAEL   I don't know.

(ELIZABETH *looks through her neatly ordered programmes.*)

ELIZABETH   Ninety-two. Ninety-two. Ninety-two. Ah ha, here we are.

(*She pulls out five for* West Side Story *and holds one up.*)

Remember this? I might have your autograph. We may have actually met before.

MICHAEL   I'd be surprised.

ELIZABETH   I've got quite a collection. Always hanging around stage doors, I was. They could be quite valuable one day.

(*She opens a programme.*)

ELIZABETH   There doesn't seem to be a photo.

MICHAEL   It was the last minute. There would have been a change of cast slip.

(*She flicks through the programmes and shakes out the pages. Nothing.*)

ELIZABETH   Oh well.

(*She puts the programmes on the desk.*)

MICHAEL   I'm sure I'd have remembered you.

ELIZABETH   Amongst all that crowd? Michael, you're trying to flatter me. (*Then she remembers the wheelchair.*) Oh, I see what you mean.

MICHAEL   I'm sorry.

ELIZABETH   No, no this was before. You know, I suddenly feel quite nervous. To think that I have a star here. A star to read my play.

MICHAEL   Hardly a star.

ELIZABETH   You were terrific.

MICHAEL   You didn't see me.

ELIZABETH   Oh, I'm sure you must have been. The chorus were excellent. All of them. Every single one. I'll tell you what, I shall acquiesce to the star's demands and we'll start at the beginning.

MICHAEL   Usually the best place to begin.

ELIZABETH   The problem with the beginning is that it is not yet finished – at least, I feel it needs rewriting.

MICHAEL   Let's just try what you've got.

ELIZABETH   I thought I'd wait for you to arrive and observe what really happened.

MICHAEL   (*sceptical*) You intend to write what we just did?

ELIZABETH   Don't be shy. It's been very useful. You don't mind if I take notes?

MICHAEL   But you can't just write down an arbitrary sequence of events and hope that just because they actually happened, they will stand up dramatically.

ELIZABETH   You don't think so?

MICHAEL   Of course not. I mean look at this.

(*He holds up his injured hand.*)

ELIZABETH Yes?

MICHAEL It was a pure accident.

ELIZABETH Oh, I don't believe in accidents.

MICHAEL You don't *believe* in them?

ELIZABETH I believe all accidents could be avoided.

MICHAEL How?

ELIZABETH With a little thought, a little care, a little consideration for others. Everything has a cause, you see. And every cause can be traced back. In the end you'll find someone is always responsible. One has to be very careful because ultimately everything one does is significant.

MICHAEL All the more reason then that you must select something more relevant.

ELIZABETH To what?

MICHAEL To the play, to your themes, to what you have to say.

ELIZABETH And your finger is not relevant?

MICHAEL No. Let's just do what you've got.

ELIZABETH Well, all right, if you think it's best.

(*She hands him a script. He takes it and sits down.*)

MICHAEL Does it have a title?

ELIZABETH "A Forced Exchange."

MICHAEL "A Forced Exchange."

ELIZABETH Like in chess. If you can think of anything better I'm open to suggestions.

MICHAEL "A Forced Exchange," a play by Elizabeth Bartlett. "Act One. A richly furnished room of a large Victorian house. Evening. Upstage, a door to the hall. Stage right, large windows with heavy curtains. Downstage right, a comfortable armchair."

(*As he reads he recognises his surroundings and motions with his hands, pointing out each feature as it is described.*)

"On the wall, downstage right, hangs a mirror. Upstage left, a cupboard. Downstage left, a wooden desk. Off-centre a small table. Furniture is well spaced to allow freedom of movement for Liz's wheelchair. The walls are decorated with framed theatrical posters and playbills. And the shelves (up and down left) are lined with books and programmes."

"Liz sits in her wheel chair adjusting her make-up. Whilst her legs are useless, she has complete use of both arms. She has about her an air of serenity and dignity. Estelle enters carrying two revolvers and a large busted tailor's dummy."

(MICHAEL *stands and blocks Estelle's movements as he reads them out.*)

"She is about twenty-five, blonde and quite beautiful."

ELIZABETH *Quite* beautiful. I mean it as a superlative.

MICHAEL Of course. *Quite* beautiful. "Estelle places the dummy in front of the windows, upstage of the the armchair."

LIZ A little more this way.

MICHAEL "Estelle obliges."

LIZ Stop. Fine. Good.

MICHAEL "Estelle places the guns in the drawer of the desk. Then she crosses to the cupboard and straightens the picture on the wall next to it. It is an aerial photograph of Brighton."

(MICHAEL *seems surprised. He looks over at the photograph.*)

ELIZABETH What?

MICHAEL No, nothing. Sorry. "Footsteps are heard on the gravel outside."

LIZ Ah ha! That's our man.

MICHAEL "Liz puts away her make-up and composes herself. Estelle heads towards the door."

LIZ Make sure you put your hat on and pull your scarf right up first.

MICHAEL (*as Estelle*) Yes, Missus Bartlett.

LIZ And . . .

MICHAEL (*as Estelle*) Yes, Missus Bartlett?

LIZ Did you lock the cupboard?

MICHAEL (*as Estelle*) Yes, Missus Bartlett.

LIZ Come here.

MICHAEL "Liz embraces her."

LIZ Thank you.

MICHAEL "The door bell rings."

LIZ Off you go. And remember, wrap up well.

MICHAEL "Estelle exits through the door." Is there any other exit from here?

ELIZABETH Only the windows.

MICHAEL Then "through the door" is not really necessary.

(ELIZABETH, *amused by his earnestness, crosses it out.*)

MICHAEL "Estelle exits to answer it. Enter Mike."

(MICHAEL *switches character and begins blocking Mike's movements.*)

"He is tall, dark and . . .

(*He pauses to look at* ELIZABETH, *amused and flattered.*)

MICHAEL ". . . breathtakingly handsome. Liz has her back to him. She seems to be having difficulty with her wheelchair."

MIKE Hello?

LIZ Mike, is that you? Mike Boyd?

MIKE How are you?

LIZ You'll have to come round.

MIKE Can I help?

LIZ It's this blasted catch. It's forever getting stuck. Would you mind?

MICHAEL "Mike bends down at the side of the wheelchair. Liz points."

LIZ Just there.

MIKE Right.

LIZ	You need to get your nails under it and pull.
MICHAEL	"Mike tries and strains."
LIZ	Bit of a bugger, isn't it?
MICHAEL	"Mike repositions himself and uses both hands."
MIKE	I think if I can . . .
MICHAEL	"It suddenly comes free."
LIZ	Ah ha! There we are.
MICHAEL	"Liz wheels left and right to demonstrate her rediscovered mobility."
LIZ	Thank you.
MICHAEL	"She takes his hands and gazes up at him."
LIZ	You know I . . .
MICHAEL	"She looks at her hands and the side of her chair."
LIZ	"There's blood on the wheel."
MIKE	My God.
LIZ	Is it you or me?
MICHAEL	This is incredible.
LIZ	Are you all right? I think it's you.
	(*Pause.*)
ELIZABETH	Michael.
MICHAEL	But I don't understand.
ELIZABETH	I would ask you to stick to what is written.

44 ACT ONE

MICHAEL "She takes out a handkerchief."

MIKE But I didn't . . .

LIZ Come here.

MICHAEL "She takes his left hand and dabs at it."

LIZ Must have been the brake.

MIKE I don't . . .

LIZ Use this.

ELIZABETH Michael?

MICHAEL "Using his right hand he grips the handkerchief on to his left hand. Liz wheels over to the desk to get some plasters."

LIZ Hold it tight. Does it hurt?

MIKE Yes.

LIZ Loosen your watch.

MICHAEL Is this some sort of game?

ELIZABETH That's not your line.

MICHAEL You're saying exactly what you said when I arrived.

ELIZABETH Isn't it fascinating?

MICHAEL You couldn't possibly have known.

ELIZABETH I would prefer it if you waited until the end of the passage.

MICHAEL It's a trick.

ELIZABETH	Michael, please. If you wish to talk about it, you may do so in a moment. In the meantime, I would be grateful if you would concentrate on the text.
LIZ	Loosen your watch.
	(MICHAEL *goes over to his jacket, takes out his watch and puts it back on.*)
ELIZABETH	Michael . . . "Loosen your watch."
MIKE	Rather tricky.
LIZ	Here, let me.
MICHAEL	"Liz unstraps his watch and places it on the table."
LIZ	Now let's have a look.
MICHAEL	"Mike holds out his hand for Liz to examine."
LIZ	Not squeamish are you? Ah ha, there we are. My goodness, so much blood for such a little scratch. You must have a strong heart.
MICHAEL	"She puts his hand on the table and squeezes out some antiseptic cream."
LIZ	A little bit of this . . .
MICHAEL	"She applies it. Mike flinches."
LIZ	Cold?
MIKE	Yes.
MICHAEL	"Liz prepares a plaster and applies it."
LIZ	"Will all great Neptune's ocean wash this blood clean from my hand?"
ELIZABETH	Now, you had something you wanted to say.

MICHAEL I think it's extraordinary.

ELIZABETH Thank you.

(*He examines his hand.*)

MICHAEL You knew I'd cut myself.

ELIZABETH Not at all.

MICHAEL It's written here.

ELIZABETH Only because I thought it would be more interesting dramatically than polite hellos.

MICHAEL I don't believe you.

ELIZABETH You are not suggesting that I foresaw it?

MICHAEL And surely you're not suggesting that it's coincidence.

ELIZABETH Sometimes it's easier to come to terms with coincidence when you think about all the coincidences that don't happen. It is the sign of an irrational mind to be astounded by coincidences.

MICHAEL But it's down here word for word.

ELIZABETH No it isn't. Not word for word.

MICHAEL But it's pretty damn close. How did you know I wouldn't refuse to help you?

ELIZABETH That's hardly likely, is it?

MICHAEL What if I hadn't cut myself?

ELIZABETH Michael, I feel that you are trying to credit me with supernatural powers. It is quite possible that you would not have cut yourself, in which case, you would think nothing of this.

MICHAEL	I think you set me up. I think you cut me on purpose.
ELIZABETH	Oh, come now, do you seriously think I'd inflict bodily harm on a guest?
MICHAEL	What's this then?

(*He holds up his hand.*)

ELIZABETH	What do you think it is?
MICHAEL	My bloody hand, that's what it is. My throbbing bloody hand.
ELIZABETH	Throbbing? Now that's interesting. Are you sure?
MICHAEL	Of course I'm sure.
ELIZABETH	So you are saying that it is a plaster soaked in blood oozing from a cut you didn't feel?
MICHAEL	What is this!
ELIZABETH	Well?
MICHAEL	Of course I felt it.
ELIZABETH	But you didn't notice it 'til later.
MICHAEL	So?
ELIZABETH	So then there is no chance it's a plaster soaked in artificial blood on a wound that doesn't exist.
MICHAEL	No.

(*Then it sinks in.* MICHAEL *examines his hand. He pulls the plaster off and looks closer. He licks a finger and wipes away the dried "blood."*)

MICHAEL	My God.

ELIZABETH You are, may I say, very open to suggestion. Actors generally are. It's the sign of a good imagination.

MICHAEL You tricked me.

ELIZABETH A little fake blood, a tiny adhesive prosthetic, the suggestion of a mechanism. My goodness, Michael, you even said it hurt. I am interested, did you really feel the pain or were you trying for a little extra sympathy?

MICHAEL You had a blood capsule in your hand.

ELIZABETH Yes.

MICHAEL And when you took my hand . . .

ELIZABETH Yes.

MICHAEL (*crestfallen*) And I didn't even notice.

ELIZABETH Oh Michael, you're making me feel terrible. Have another drink.

MICHAEL No thank you.

ELIZABETH Well, if you're sure.

MICHAEL Why?

ELIZABETH . . . did I trick you?

MICHAEL Yes.

ELIZABETH You don't mind if I . . . ?

(*She holds up the bottle of Scotch and pours herself another glass.*)

ELIZABETH I had to check it was actually possible to convince a man he'd sustained a non-existent cut.

MICHAEL Why?

ELIZABETH   For the sake of the play.

MICHAEL   But why in the play?

ELIZABETH   As part of the plan.

MICHAEL   The plan?

ELIZABETH   To unsettle him.

MICHAEL   Him?

ELIZABETH   Mike. My Mike. I needed to know if it was credible.

MICHAEL   What if I'd sucked it?

ELIZABETH   Yes?

MICHAEL   Then I'd have realised.

ELIZABETH   True. But forestalled quite effectively by the line, "Is it you or me?" don't you think? I doubt somehow that anyone would suck blood from their hand if there was the slightest suspicion that the blood was not their own.

MICHAEL   You said that you didn't know I would cut myself. You said it was quite possible that I could have arrived here and not cut myself. But you knew all along.

ELIZABETH   So?

MICHAEL   So you were lying.

ELIZABETH   Please, Michael. Remember you *didn't* cut yourself. I think, in fairness, such an accusation is unfounded.

MICHAEL   And how do you intend that Mike becomes unsettled?

ELIZABETH	When it is shown that he has been deceived.
MICHAEL	Just as I have been shown.
ELIZABETH	That is unfortunate.
MICHAEL	And so my feelings are to be disregarded.
ELIZABETH	I am paying you very handsomely. Handsome pay for a handsome man.
MICHAEL	Not to be experimented on.
ELIZABETH	How *do* you feel?
MICHAEL	I come here in good faith. I help you with your wheelchair. I indulge you. I act out your scenes. And then I find it's all part of some elaborate trick.
ELIZABETH	Come and sit down.

(MICHAEL *turns away, refusing.* ELIZABETH *wheels closer and looks up at him.*)

ELIZABETH   I didn't appreciate that it would be quite so distressing. I thought you might find it rather amusing. My apologies. If it is any consolation, your contribution has been most enlightening. Will you forgive me?

MICHAEL   I think I will have that drink.

ELIZABETH   Of course. Please.

(*She motions him to help himself. He goes over to the drinks cabinet and pours himself a large Scotch.*)

ELIZABETH   I'm curious. If Stephen Barlow was unable to perform for a whole year following his overdose, and you were his understudy, why did you only appear for one week?

MICHAEL   You let me feel guilty about your dress.

ELIZABETH   Yes, I'm sorry. Now *I* feel guilty.

             (*Pause.*)

ELIZABETH   Perhaps from now on we should just stick to the key passages.

MICHAEL   And miss out what?

ELIZABETH   Nothing of much consequence.

MICHAEL   Passages of little consequence should be eliminated.

ELIZABETH   Except we do learn something about Liz's background.

MICHAEL   Oh?

ELIZABETH   She was a ballet dancer.

MICHAEL   Really?

ELIZABETH   At Covent Garden.

MICHAEL   And that is important?

ELIZABETH   Vital.

MICHAEL   I imagine being confined to a wheelchair must have been all the more frustrating.

ELIZABETH   Exactly.

MICHAEL   To have been trained in movement, to have had freedom and to lose it.

ELIZABETH   I knew you would understand.

MICHAEL   And?

ELIZABETH   What?

MICHAEL   What else do we learn about her?

ELIZABETH   That she was elbowed out of the company when she was only twenty-nine. That she took up teaching and surprised herself by enjoying it enormously. That she snared a rich old husband who took her to every West End opening night. That he died but her passion for theatre did not. And that those evenings in London and the classes she taught kept her going. Gave her a sense of purpose.

(*She flicks through the script.*)

ELIZABETH   Now let's see. How about the top of page thirty?

(MICHAEL *finds it.*)

MICHAEL   "Liz sits in her wheelchair adjusting her make-up. Whilst her legs are useless she has full use of both arms . . . and so on, and so on.

ELIZABETH   (*clearing her throat*) Excuse me?

MICHAEL   Surely . . . I mean unless you want me to repeat . . . ?

ELIZABETH   This isn't repetition. This time you aren't reading the stage directions, Mike is. Mike is an actor. He's come to read a part in a play. In this play he plays a character not unlike himself, called Mick. Liz plays someone, not unlike herself, called Liza. Try to . . .

MICHAEL   Hold it, hold it. I, Michael, am playing Mike who is reading the part of Mick?

ELIZABETH   Exactly.

MICHAEL   And you, Elizabeth, are playing Liz who is reading the part of Liza.

ELIZABETH   It's actually much more simple than it sounds. Mike is now in the position you were a little earlier. It may help you to draw on that experience as you read.

(*Pause while* MICHAEL *takes it in*.)

ELIZABETH OK?

MICHAEL No. I don't know.

ELIZABETH Just try it.

MIKE "She has about her an air of serenity and dignity. She applies make-up from a compact. Estelle enters carrying two revolvers and a large-busted tailor's dummy. She is about twenty-five, blonde and (*Up.*) *quite* beautiful."

ELIZABETH No, no, no. (*Down.*) *Quite* beautiful.

MICHAEL But you said . . .

ELIZABETH You're supposed to get it wrong.

MICHAEL Am I?

ELIZABETH Like you did.

MIKE And (*Down.*) *quite* beautiful.

LIZ (*up*) *Quite* beautiful. I mean it as a superlative.

(MICHAEL *is irritated*.)

MIKE Of course. (*Up.*) "*Quite* beautiful. She places the dummy in front of the windows, upstage of the armchair."

LIZA A little more this way.

MIKE "Estelle obliges."

LIZA Stop. Fine. Good.

MIKE	"Estelle places the guns in the drawer of the desk. Then she crosses to the cupboard and straightens the picture on the wall next to it. It is an aerial photograph of Brighton."
MICHAEL	This is amazing.
ELIZABETH	What?
MICHAEL	This next line: "That's where I was born." Because I was.
LIZ	How strange.

(*He stands up to take a closer look.*)

MICHAEL	And this next one because, look, that *is* the house. Just like it says. You knew didn't you?
ELIZABETH	Please stick to what is written.
MICHAEL	Is this part of "the plan", too?

(MICHAEL *flicks through the script.*)

ELIZABETH	Please go on.
MICHAEL	No, I'm sorry.
ELIZABETH	This is a very important moment.
MICHAEL	Good God, you've got it all here.
ELIZABETH	Michael, we've been through this.
MICHAEL	But don't you see. This is different.
ELIZABETH	If you wish to talk about it you may do so in a moment. In the meantime, I would be grateful if you would concentrate on the text.
MICHAEL	Are you reading that or telling me?

ELIZABETH   Are you going to continue or not? No? Very well. (*She reads.*) "Mike looks up from his script and we realise that what is real and what is written is no longer clearly defined. Sometimes the characters read from the script. Other times they appear to be speaking for themselves. The two blend together so that the words of each person and their character form a coherent progression as if the product of one mind."

MICHAEL   Bullshit!

ELIZABETH   But don't you see what's happening?

MICHAEL   What the hell is this?

ELIZABETH   What the hell is what?

MICHAEL   This! This whole bloody charade.

ELIZABETH   Please, Michael.

MICHAEL   You're trying to . . .

ELIZABETH   What? Upset you?

MICHAEL   Yes.

ELIZABETH   Really, you're putting words in my mouth.

MICHAEL   Oh, *I'm* putting words in *your* mouth?!

ELIZABETH   You must try to distinguish between yourself and the character you are playing. It is quite simple: there is us; the play we are reading; and the play the characters are reading. Do try not to get confused.

(*She wheels over to the drinks and holds up the Scotch.*)

ELIZABETH   More?

MICHAEL   No thank you.

ELIZABETH I think I might call it "A Determined Young Man."

(*No response.*)

What can I do?

(*No response.*)

I do hope you aren't thinking about giving up.

(*She pours him some Scotch and hands it to him. He ignores her and so she sets it down on the table near by.*)

I wouldn't want to force you of course, but it would be so disappointing.

(MICHAEL *begins to nod and smile to himself as if beginning to understand.*)

Michael?

MICHAEL How did you do it? How did you write this?

ELIZABETH That's more like it!

MICHAEL Brian told you, didn't he?

ELIZABETH Brian?

MICHAEL Sacks. My agent. He told you where I was born.

ELIZABETH How else could I have known?

MICHAEL But why did you ask him?

ELIZABETH I didn't. It just cropped up.

MICHAEL And you went to all the trouble of finding a picture.

ELIZABETH Actually, it was no trouble. I've had the picture for years. When I heard where you were born I thought it might be interesting to see your reaction.

MICHAEL But how did you know I'd tell you I was born there? I could have seen the picture and said nothing.

ELIZABETH As indeed you did.

MICHAEL What?

ELIZABETH I think, if you recall, on our first run through you actually said nothing when the picture was mentioned. You paused and you glanced over at it but you said nothing. You only told me you were born there after you'd read it in the script. More cause than prediction I'd say.

MICHAEL But what about the rest of it?

(*He sets the script down on the table and turns the pages.*)

Mick cuts his finger just as Mike did and just as I did. Mike is astounded just as I was. How did you do it? How on earth did you do it?

ELIZABETH It has gone rather well, hasn't it?

MICHAEL You've been manipulating me all evening.

ELIZABETH Oh, please.

MICHAEL Think of a number between one and ten.

ELIZABETH Seven.

MICHAEL No don't tell me.

ELIZABETH OK, I've got another.

MICHAEL Multiply it by nine.

ELIZABETH OK.

MICHAEL Add the digits. Take away three.

ELIZABETH And I'm left with six. Of course. You see, you understand perfectly.

MICHAEL But it's not that simple. Yes, I'm here at your request. Yes, I am here to oblige. And yes I have little room for initiative . . .

ELIZABETH Except now.

MICHAEL What?

ELIZABETH Now you are exercising your own independence.

MICHAEL (*disconcerted*) I'll be absolutely honest with you. I am impressed.

ELIZABETH And?

MICHAEL I would like an explanation.

ELIZABETH Would an explanation make you feel better?

MICHAEL It would make me feel . . . less . . .

ELIZABETH What if there is no explanation?

MICHAEL Oh, for God's sake.

ELIZABETH You are a highly predictable animal. And I am a very intuitive woman. Enough knowledge about your background and character has enabled me to anticipate your every move.

MICHAEL You know nothing about my background and character.

ELIZABETH On the contrary. Mr Sacks was most forthcoming. Though I must admit he was rather reticent when it came to *West Side Story*. Why was that, Michael? I would have thought an agent would be keen to advertise his client's success. Assuming it was a success.

MICHAEL It's not important.

ELIZABETH Oh, but it's terribly important.

MICHAEL We are getting away from the point.

ELIZABETH Which is?

MICHAEL Even within the limits you are talking about there is an infinity of possibilities. You can't know in advance.

ELIZABETH Not true. The future is what you make it.

(*She picks up her glass.*)

ELIZABETH This glass. What can we know about its future? We could make vague guesses. Sooner or later it is bound to be washed – later if Estelle has anything to do with it. And probably it will be put back up on the shelf. Or, we can say that in five seconds it will be smashed to pieces.

(*She holds it up ready to drop it.*)

ELIZABETH Do you get my point Michael? Five, four, three, two . . .

(MICHAEL *springs forward and wrests the glass from her. He holds it up in triumph.*)

MICHAEL There, you see!

ELIZABETH He holds it up in triumph. A symbol of his independence and freedom.

MICHAEL And now you're going to tell me you've got this written down, too.

(Michael *makes to pick up his script but* Elizabeth *beats him to it and holds it close to her chest.*)

Elizabeth: Am I?

Michael: Give it to me.

Elizabeth: If you don't wish to continue, I don't feel you deserve to see it.

Michael: Then perhaps I'll go.

(*He picks up his jacket.*)

Michael: Unless you've got the door locked, too?

(*He tries the handle. But he can't get it open.*)

Elizabeth: Oh Michael, really.

(*She wheels over and calmly opens it for him.*)

Elizabeth: Believe me you're free to walk out of here any time you choose.

(*He makes to leave and then stops in the doorway.*)

Michael: I'll have my money now if you don't mind.

Elizabeth: Actually, I do mind. But if that's the way you want it.

(*She wheels over to the desk.*)

Elizabeth: Your presence has been most instructive so I am prepared to give you half your fee.

(*She looks over at him for a reaction. He snorts and looks away.*)

Elizabeth: I must confess that I had hoped to have excited your curiosity as to the outcome.

MICHAEL   I'll take it.

             (*She puts the scripts down on the desk next to the* West Side Story *programmes and takes out a cheque book.*)

ELIZABETH   A cheque is OK I hope, or would you prefer cash?

MICHAEL   A cheque is all right.

ELIZABETH   You trust me not to run down to the bank in the morning and have it stopped. Oh dear.

             (*She holds up the cheque book. Empty.*)

ELIZABETH   I'm afraid it's going to have to be cash after all. Back in a mo'.

             (*She exits leaving the door open.* MICHAEL *waits until she is out of sight. Then he tosses his jacket on to the armchair and runs over to the desk to look at the scripts. He is distracted by the sight of the* West Side Story *programmes lying on the desk. He picks one up and flicks through it. A slip of paper falls out. He picks it up and reads it. The lights come down.*)

ACT TWO

MICHAEL *stands next to the armchair with his back to the open door.* ELIZABETH *enters carrying two boxes, a white one and a black one.* MICHAEL *appears to be thinking.*

ELIZABETH   Michael?

(*He seems not to notice.*)

ELIZABETH   I've got your money. It's all right here.

(MICHAEL *turns, slowly, calmly. There is a hint of a smile on his lips.* ELIZABETH *watches him, puzzled. He closes the door and circles her chair.*)

ELIZABETH   Michael? Michael?

(MICHAEL *stops in front of her, arms folded and looks down at her.*)

MICHAEL   What's this all about, Elizabeth?

ELIZABETH   I don't know what you mean.

MICHAEL   I mean: What's this all about, Elizabeth?

ELIZABETH   Well I'm about to give you some money for your services. Two hundred pounds, I think we said. And I expect shortly we're going to . . .

MICHAEL   What?

ELIZABETH   . . . be saying goodbye.

MICHAEL   Are we?

ELIZABETH   Well, yes. Aren't we? Of course if you want to stay, I'd be more than happy.

MICHAEL   Yes, I bet you would.

ELIZABETH	Well yes, I would. Really. What's this about?
MICHAEL	Ah, no, that's my question.
ELIZABETH	Shall we sort out the money then?
MICHAEL	I've got a better idea.
ELIZABETH	Yes?
MICHAEL	Why don't you tell me what this is?
	(*He holds up the slip of paper from the programme.* ELIZABETH *reaches out for it but* MICHAEL *pulls it just out of reach.*)
MICHAEL	Uh-uh.
ELIZABETH	Well, I've really no idea.
MICHAEL	Oh, I think you have. (*Reading from the slip.*) "The management regrets . . ." (*He looks to see if she recognises it.*) No? ". . . that Stephen Barlow is indisposed. In tonight's performance the part of Tony will be played by . . ." any idea?
	(*He hands it to her.*)
ELIZABETH	Well that's quite extraordinary. Where did that come from?
MICHAEL	Well, gosh, I have no idea.
ELIZABETH	It was in the programme.
MICHAEL	Was it?
ELIZABETH	It must have been. My goodness. So that means . . .
MICHAEL	Yes?
ELIZABETH	That apart from the fact you've been going through my things . . .

MICHAEL   Yes?

ELIZABETH   Well it means that I was mistaken.

MICHAEL   In that . . . ?

ELIZABETH   I must have seen you as Tony.

MICHAEL   How extraordinary. Or . . .

ELIZABETH   What?

MICHAEL   It means something else.

ELIZABETH   I'm sorry, I don't follow.

MICHAEL   That you have been telling a few little fibs.

ELIZABETH   I don't know what you mean.

MICHAEL   Oh, come on. You knew very well that you'd seen me.

ELIZABETH   No. I was mistaken.

MICHAEL   But you're so keen on detail. My agent told me you'd given him a very specific description of the actor you wanted this evening. No name, but a precise physical description – somebody, in fact, looking very much like me. He'd suggested a couple of others because it didn't pay well, but you turned them down and upped the fee. And that's when he sent me.

ELIZABETH   So?

MICHAEL   So I think you've got a thing about me.

ELIZABETH   Oh, Michael. You're very charming, I'm sure. But really.

MICHAEL   So you had no idea I was coming tonight.

ELIZABETH Well, no. I mean I knew someone called Michael Boyd was coming but the name meant nothing to me.

MICHAEL So it could equally well have been somebody else here tonight.

ELIZABETH If they looked the part, yes.

MICHAEL Oh, by the way I worked out what Estelle meant.

ELIZABETH About what?

MICHAEL When I arrived. Not placard. Placard. It's French.

ELIZABETH Is it? My French is not up to much.

MICHAEL For cupboard.

ELIZABETH Are you sure?

MICHAEL She was telling me to look in the cupboard.

ELIZABETH But why on earth . . .

MICHAEL Perhaps because she wanted me to find this.

(*He takes out a scrapbook from the cupboard.*)

ELIZABETH This is outrageous. How dare you pry into a locked cupboard.

MICHAEL Oh, but it wasn't locked.

ELIZABETH I distinctly told her.

MICHAEL And she indistinctly told me.

ELIZABETH The treacherous little tart.

MICHAEL Elizabeth.

ELIZABETH And you're not much better.

MICHAEL	(*turning the pages*) Every cutting, every tiny clip since *West Side Story*. Some of these I haven't even seen myself.
ELIZABETH	Put it back. Michael, put it away.
MICHAEL	I'll ask you once again. What's this all about, Elizabeth?
ELIZABETH	All right if you insist on humiliating me. Yes I think you are a . . . very . . . attractive person. I have done since I first laid eyes on you. This is so embarrassing.

(MICHAEL *draws up a chair.*)

MICHAEL	Go on. I understand.
ELIZABETH	Yes I bet this happens to you all the time doesn't it – silly women getting crushes.
MICHAEL	When did you first "lay your eyes" on me? At *West Side Story*?
ELIZABETH	When you came on stage, I felt a fluttering in my stomach like I hadn't had since I was sixteen. It was so unexpected and so . . . well it was . . . I liked it, Michael. You made me feel alive again. I didn't really watch your performance. I just watched you. Afterwards I ran round to the stage door. I wanted to be first in line to congratulate you and get your autograph.
MICHAEL	But?
ELIZABETH	What?
MICHAEL	What went wrong?
ELIZABETH	Well I missed out, didn't I. "Not to worry," I thought, "always tomorrow" – if I could get tickets. Even if I couldn't, I thought I'd come along anyway. But of course, as it turned out, I never made it.

MICHAEL   Why not?

ELIZABETH   For the same reason I've not been to any performances anywhere since.

MICHAEL   What happened?

ELIZABETH   Can't you guess? You know, I'll probably get nightmares again. It was a car. A taxi, actually. I was in it and well . . .

MICHAEL   It crashed?

ELIZABETH   It's so maddening sometimes – can't do anything for myself. Poor Estelle, I tend to take it out on her.

MICHAEL   Were you really a dancer?

ELIZABETH   Oh, yes. Great days. Which makes it worse now, I think. Or am I just being selfish?

MICHAEL   So you saw me in one performance and ever since you've been a fan?

ELIZABETH   Not "a fan", please. I hate that word. Fan, fanatic – makes me sound like a lunatic.

MICHAEL   How would you describe yourself?

ELIZABETH   I don't mind "obsessed".

MICHAEL   (*laughs*) OK. So since that one performance you've been obsessed.

ELIZABETH   Yes.

MICHAEL   By me.

ELIZABETH   You have to understand – it was a momentous day. It's not every day you develop feelings for someone and later get paralysed from the waist down.

MICHAEL   A crush and a crash.

ELIZABETH   Please don't make light of it, Michael.

MICHAEL   And since that day you've followed my career.

ELIZABETH   I was in a coma for a while. But once I'd recovered, yes. I've followed all your ups and downs. And let's be honest – I'm not completely blind to it – there have been some downs.

MICHAEL   And you decided to write a play, or part of a play as an excuse to get to meet me.

ELIZABETH   Well I did consider writing to you. But it didn't seem appropriate. "Dear Mr Boyd, or may I call you Michael. I am an obsessed admirer of yours. Would you like to come to tea so that I can show you my scrapbook and maybe later we can get cosy."

                (*She screws up her face in disapproval.*)

MICHAEL   The kiss.

ELIZABETH   Ah, yes.

MICHAEL   So you *were* getting off on it.

ELIZABETH   Oh, that sounds so sleazy.

MICHAEL   You were taking advantage.

ELIZABETH   Don't hate me, please.

MICHAEL   Hate you? I don't hate you. I just . . .

ELIZABETH   What?

MICHAEL   Want to understand.

ELIZABETH   I must say, now it's out in the open it's a relief. But I suppose it's also the death of hope, isn't it?

	We're never going to be . . . are we? We're never going to . . .
MICHAEL	Why didn't you at least admit to having seen me once?
ELIZABETH	Because we'd have ended up talking about it and I'd have ended up telling you I was . . . or rather you'd have got the impression that I was infatuated with you.
MICHAEL	Which you didn't want.
ELIZABETH	I wanted us to be on an equal footing.
MICHAEL	But there are so many other things we could have done this evening. Why choose what you did?
ELIZABETH	I had to choose something.
MICHAEL	Why not something more straightforward?
ELIZABETH	I didn't want it to be boring. And I certainly didn't want you patronising me.
MICHAEL	You had me kiss you, you tricked me, you tried to rattle me.
ELIZABETH	I don't suppose you would . . . (*She holds up the programme and pen so he can sign.*) . . . seeing as I missed you the first time.
MICHAEL	Not until you tell me why.
ELIZABETH	Please.
MICHAEL	No.
ELIZABETH	If you sign it then I'll tell you anything you want to know.
	(MICHAEL *hesitates*.)
ELIZABETH	Honestly. Anything.

MICHAEL   You'll explain all about this evening.

ELIZABETH If that's what you want. Promise. Guide's honour.

           (MICHAEL *takes the programme and gets a pen from the desk.*)

MICHAEL   You know I don't trust you for one moment.

ELIZABETH Oh don't be like that.

           (MICHAEL *signs.*)

ELIZABETH There that wasn't so hard was it? Hardly took a moment. Eh, Michael? Easiest thing in the world. Don't you agree?

MICHAEL   What?

ELIZABETH Don't you agree that signing an autograph is the easiest thing in the world. It's really just a matter of manners. Doesn't cost anything.

           (MICHAEL *stares at her, struck by a frightening thought.*)

MICHAEL   Oh my God.

ELIZABETH What?

MICHAEL   Why didn't you get my autograph?

ELIZABETH Well I tried. I told you.

MICHAEL   But why didn't you get it?

ELIZABETH Well I don't know. You must have had things on your mind. They must have been heady moments. What would you want with me?

MICHAEL   You were there but I walked past.

ELIZABETH   You had a girl with you. I expect you were off to
            . . . have a good time.

MICHAEL   Oh my God. Oh my God.

ELIZABETH   What is it?

MICHAEL   You blame me.

ELIZABETH   What?

MICHAEL   For your accident. You blame me. I come out late.
            You've been waiting. I ignore you. You get a taxi
            home, which crashes. And so I'm responsible.

ELIZABETH   Is that an admission?

(MICHAEL *stares at her, horrified.*)

ELIZABETH   Michael, I don't blame you. Of course I don't. It
            was just a coincidence.

MICHAEL   And we both know what you think about
            coincidence. Everything we've been doing. Good
            God, everything.

ELIZABETH   What?

MICHAEL   Has been for a reason.

ELIZABETH   The play.

MICHAEL   No, not the play. It's not a play. It didn't even
            have an ending until I arrived. It's just bits and
            pieces. First the kiss because you fancy me. Then
            the guns. You were getting off on that, too.

ELIZABETH   Oh, Michael.

MICHAEL   Yes you were. I saw you. What was it, some
            bizarre catharsis? I bet you actually have had
            suicidal thoughts. And I bet you've fantasised
            about me pulling the trigger. I saw you when we
            did it. For you that was real.

ELIZABETH   Really, this is very interesting but . . .

MICHAEL   And what about the rest of it? What did you say it was about?

ELIZABETH   I didn't say it was about anything.

MICHAEL   Your themes, what were they?

ELIZABETH   Oh those. Well "freedom" was one.

MICHAEL   Yes, freedom. And . . .

ELIZABETH   If you want me to look them up . . .

MICHAEL   Freedom, identity, empowerment. Yes, I get it. That's what the finger was all about. You pull this strange trick and try and persuade me that you've predicted my actions. You thought you could spook me.

ELIZABETH   And I did.

MICHAEL   Then you admit it.

ELIZABETH   Michael, I just wrote what interests me. If you insist on looking for deeper reasons . . .

MICHAEL   You feel you've lost your freedom – your physical freedom. And you've lost your identity because you used to dance and now you can't. So you try to take them away from me too. Why me? Because there is no one else. It was an accident but you don't believe in accidents. You can't bear to believe that no one is responsible so you fix on me. But it's all tricks. You haven't taken away my freedom.

ELIZABETH   I have one more trick to play.

MICHAEL   Let me ask you, Elizabeth. Forget all the bullshit and the evasions. Look at me. Do you really think I'm to blame? Do you?

ELIZABETH   Do you?

MICHAEL   Of course not. I mean I'm sorry you had your accident. And I'm sorry I didn't give you an autograph.

ELIZABETH   Are you?

MICHAEL   Of course I am. I didn't ignore you on purpose. It certainly wasn't my intention to hurt your feelings.

ELIZABETH   But you had things on your mind.

MICHAEL   Yes, I did have things on my mind. But the point is that I am not responsible. Jesus. If I was I might as well admit responsibility for every other bad thing that's ever happened. Don't you see – it's absurd. I am not to blame, am I?

ELIZABETH   I think we should sort out the money.

MICHAEL   Answer me.

(*She stares at him, stony faced.*)

MICHAEL   Answer me!

(*No response.*)

MICHAEL   (*exasperated*) All right yes, give me the money. Come on. Give it and I'll go.

ELIZABETH   It's in one of these.

MICHAEL   Don't play games with me.

ELIZABETH   Actually it's in here.

(*She hands him the white box. He tries to open it but it is locked.*)

ELIZABETH   I'm going to give you a choice.

MICHAEL   No you're not. You're going to give me the key. I'm going to take the money and then I'm going to go.

ELIZABETH   Yes, but hear me out first please.

MICHAEL   No.

ELIZABETH   It's worth another hundred.

MICHAEL   No.

ELIZABETH   Two hundred?

(MICHAEL *hesitates*.)

ELIZABETH   That'll be your full fee if you just hear me out.

(*Pause.*)

MICHAEL   OK, come on then..

ELIZABETH   OK. In there (*The white box.*) there is, as I say, four hundred pounds. That's for sure. No question. Cross my heart and hope to die.

MICHAEL   And in the other?

ELIZABETH   Is something rather more interesting. It's not money. In fact it's probably quite worthless.

MICHAEL   And?

ELIZABETH   What?

MICHAEL   What is it?

ELIZABETH   Well, that's the point, you see. If you want to find out you'll have to forgo the money box and choose this one instead.

MICHAEL   But I don't want to find out.

ELIZABETH Fair enough.

(*She holds out the key.*)

MICHAEL Why would I want to find out?

(ELIZABETH *shrugs.*)

MICHAEL Why?

ELIZABETH Perhaps because it contains an interesting souvenir.

MICHAEL Of what?

(ELIZABETH *shrugs again.* MICHAEL *shakes his head, exasperated.*)

MICHAEL Sorry, not interested. Not interested.

(*He takes the key, opens the box and takes out the money. There are eight fifty pound notes. He counts it quickly, pockets it and prepares to leave.*)

ELIZABETH Don't I get a thank you?

MICHAEL Well, it's been a fascinating evening.

ELIZABETH And you'll be off.

MICHAEL I'll see myself out.

ELIZABETH Yes, I'm afraid you'll have to.

MICHAEL Yes, well. Goodnight.

ELIZABETH Safe journey.

(MICHAEL *approaches the door with suspicion. He tries the handle very deliberately. It opens easily. He exits.* ELIZABETH *sits perfectly still watching the door. We hear the front door open and close.*

ELIZABETH *waits. Then the door opens and* MICHAEL *comes back in.*)

MICHAEL   OK, OK. What's in the box?

ELIZABETH   We made a deal. We played a game.

MICHAEL   I know it's another trick but come on, have your fun.

ELIZABETH   If I open this one we'll be breaking the rules.

MICHAEL   We've played your game. Just open the box.

ELIZABETH   I'm sorry but I can't do that, Michael.

MICHAEL   OK look, how much?

(*He takes a note from his pocket.*)

ELIZABETH   I'm sorry, Michael.

(*He takes out another note.*)

ELIZABETH   Sorry.

(MICHAEL *snatches the box from her and tries the key from the white box. It does not fit.*)

ELIZABETH   OK, Michael. Here's what I can do. I'll open the box if you give me two hundred pounds *and* you promise not to lay claim to what's inside.

MICHAEL   What? If I what?

ELIZABETH   If you promise not to lay claim to what's inside.

MICHAEL   It's a photograph or something, isn't it, of me?

ELIZABETH   Maybe, maybe not.

MICHAEL   If it's a photograph, or a programme or I don't know what . . .

ELIZABETH   Perhaps it's nothing. Perhaps I'm just bluffing.

MICHAEL   OK, listen. (*He hesitates.*) Shit. I won't lay claim to what's inside but I'm not giving you back any money.

ELIZABETH   So I can keep whatever's inside? Is that a yes or a no?

MICHAEL   Yes, yes, all right.

ELIZABETH   But no money?

MICHAEL   No.

ELIZABETH   Well all right. You drive a hard bargain. Deal. If you'd like to do the honours.

(*She hands him another key. He opens the box and stops dead. He takes out a black book.*)

MICHAEL   You are a mad fucking crazy bitch. Where did you get this?

ELIZABETH   Do you recognise it?

MICHAEL   Of course I recognise it. Do you think I don't recognise my own handwriting!? How the hell did you get it?

ELIZABETH   How do *you* think?

MICHAEL   I've a good mind to go to the police.

ELIZABETH   Yes, you do.

MICHAEL   What?

ELIZABETH   Have a good mind.

MICHAEL   Jesus!

ELIZABETH   For these purposes at any rate.

MICHAEL You are a thief.

ELIZABETH Me?

MICHAEL Do you have any idea what these mean to me? They're all I have. No one's read them, ever. No one.

ELIZABETH Except me.

MICHAEL You are being reported.

ELIZABETH For what? Theft of character? Destruction of memory?

MICHAEL Breaking and entering.

ELIZABETH Me, breaking and entering?

MICHAEL Not you, her!

(*He points at the dummy.*)

ELIZABETH And when exactly did this happen?

MICHAEL You know who I mean.

ELIZABETH But is there any proof? Was the door forced? Was any damage done? Is any property missing?

MICHAEL This is missing.

ELIZABETH No it's not, it's in your hand. You could have brought it here yourself.

MICHAEL The contents, the intellectual property.

ELIZABETH *Intellectual?* – hardly. No, Michael, it's a nice idea but I have received no financial gain from your "intellectual" property and I have not tried to publish it. You cannot prove that I know what is in your diaries. And even if you could, it would not constitute theft. The law is interested in things more tangible.

(*She reaches out for the book but* MICHAEL *pulls back.*)

ELIZABETH Oh that's a pity, because there's a particularly relevant passage. March twentieth. Perhaps you would care to read it out.

(*No response.*)

Well then, I suggest you read it for yourself. Really.

(MICHAEL *hesitates and then opens the book, finds the page and reads it quickly.*)

ELIZABETH Your lips are moving.

(MICHAEL *ignores her. He begins to look puzzled. He sits down to study it more closely.*)

ELIZABETH What is it Michael? Something amiss? Why don't you read it out?

(*He ignores her.*)

ELIZABETH I wonder if I can remember – I've read, often enough: "March twentieth. Nineteen ninety-two. The dressing room. I have asked everyone to leave so that I can collect my thoughts. There is an hour to go until curtain up. I am very conscious that this is a key point in my life and I feel I should just take a moment to stand back and look at myself. If all goes well tonight who knows what might happen to me, what opportunities will present themselves. But failure could be the end of everything. This is it. I am living on the edge. It needs courage to admit these feelings. For, who knows, one day I may reread this entry and feel I failed. It is not easy to admit my hopes and ambitions for fear of failure."

MICHAEL I am not going to justify what I have written in my own *private* diary to a perfect stranger.

ELIZABETH Oh Michael, please. We're not strangers are we? Not any more. I can't remember, don't you go on to say something about that chorus girl . . . whatshername . . . Julia . . . ah yes . . . "Julia has just this moment popped her head round the door to wish me luck. I said, Thanks, and she paused, then she came in, half dressed, and as she bent down to give me a peck on the cheek, a breast fell free beneath her robe. She giggled and tucked it back in. Already I sense the possible rewards of success." Did you get your reward, Michael?

MICHAEL That's none of your fucking business.

ELIZABETH A revealing choice of words.

MICHAEL No it isn't, because I never did . . .

ELIZABETH What? Fuck Julia?

MICHAEL Have sex with her.

ELIZABETH So much more sensitive. What a pity. Beautiful, giggling, big-breasted Julia. "March twenty-third. The bedroom. Julia came back with me after the show. We drank some champagne and we smoked some dope. She saw my copy of *The Joy Of Sex* on the shelf and when we were pleasantly intoxicated, we took it down to look at. She suggested that we take off our clothes and try out all the positions illustrated in the centre. We giggled the whole time like two eight-year-olds discovering our bodies for the first time. It was the most uninhibited, erotic sex I have ever had."

MICHAEL You're making it up.

ELIZABETH March twenty-third.

(MICHAEL *finds the page and reads.*)

ELIZABETH Surely you haven't forgotten. "The most uninhibited, erotic sex I have ever had." I think I'd remember a night like that. I wish I *could* remember a night like that. Your passionate lips didn't do much for me earlier.

(MICHAEL *stands up and paces around. He is a little unsteady – the worse for the Scotch. He pours himself another.*)

ELIZABETH   You have forgotten. That's the trouble with drugs. They addle the brain. Eat away at your memory. Induce fantasy.

MICHAEL   I don't take drugs.

ELIZABETH   "We smoked some dope."

MICHAEL   I didn't write that.

ELIZABETH   Alcohol also distorts perceptions.

MICHAEL   I didn't write that!

(*Pause.*)

ELIZABETH   What are you thinking, Michael?

(*He ignores her.*)

ELIZABETH   Michael? All right then, let me guess. You are thinking: "Did I really have sex with Julia? No. Am I sure? Yes because it is inconceivable that I would have forgotten. She came back with me but we didn't have sex. Now, there are things that I have written down that I have forgotten but I'd never have forgotten that. So if I didn't do it, how come it is written down?" (*Slowly.*) Unless it is some kind of forgery.

MICHAEL   My God, I don't believe it.

ELIZABETH   But you must believe something. Either it is a forgery or you can't trust your mind. I'll have it back now please.

MICHAEL   Bollocks.

ELIZABETH   But you promised I could keep it.

(MICHAEL *holds it tight to his chest.*)

MICHAEL   You stole it. It was never yours in the first place.

ELIZABETH   But if it is a forgery, which I think you think it is, then it isn't yours. Yours is probably at home on the shelf with all the other volumes. That one is mine.

(*He holds it up to examine the cover.*)

ELIZABETH   Go ahead, be my guest.

(*He opens it and flicks through the pages.* ELIZABETH *makes a running commentary.*)

ELIZABETH   A standard blank book with hard back cover, available from Rymans, priced three pounds forty-nine. The words "December '91 to May '92" inscribed in silver ink above the number of the volume. Inside the cover a credit card pin cunningly disguised as a telephone number, and a list of numbers and dates indicating time taken for a three-mile run you undertake at irregular intervals roughly once a week. The diary runs backwards starting with the last page as page one. The first entry begins: "If I flick through these white pages they are still clean and fresh, not yet tainted by disappointment, and I feel a brief thrill, almost as if I could make a new start." As to the writing, well it certainly looks like yours, but is it yours? If it is a forgery it must have been copied directly from the original with only a few details altered.

MICHAEL   You should be locked up. For God's sake. It's unimaginable – the planning. I mean, how did you do this?

ELIZABETH Let's suppose I don't tell you. What will you do? How will you rationalise it?

MICHAEL Who did it?

ELIZABETH Who did what?

MICHAEL (*slamming the diary*) This!

ELIZABETH Simon T Brodey.

MICHAEL Who's Simon T Brodey?

ELIZABETH A master of his craft. Estelle found him.

MICHAEL After she broke into my flat.

ELIZABETH Oh, she didn't have to break in. You invited her.

MICHAEL You're a lunatic. A complete fucking lunatic.

ELIZABETH Remember I said how much she enjoyed your performance in *Three's A Crowd*? And remember that young woman you took home one night after the show – the one who virtually threw herself at you in the bar afterwards? What did she say her name was? Sophie something or other. You never found out her surname did you?

MICHAEL Jesus!

ELIZABETH You didn't even recognise her when you arrived this evening. Mind you, she was well wrapped up. And the French all sound the same don't they?

MICHAEL You're lying.

ELIZABETH Am I?

MICHAEL You sent her to sleep with me?

ELIZABETH Yes.

MICHAEL And she agreed?

ELIZABETH Oh Michael, where's your self-esteem? I'm sure it wasn't so unpleasant even though you were pissed. In the morning she snuck out and got a copy of your key, while you emerged from your drunken stupor. Came back with some coffee, remember, quick breakfast, "Thanks for a good time. See you around." After that, easy access any time you're out.

MICHAEL That's bollocks. Bollocks.

ELIZABETH Is it? Because I think with a bit of fine tuning it would be a perfectly reasonable explanation. You see, the problem is not in finding an explanation. The problem is your believing it. Alternatively, for instance . . .

MICHAEL What? What?

ELIZABETH Well, tell me, what do you know about hypnosis?

MICHAEL Bollocks.

ELIZABETH Which seems to be your favourite word.

MICHAEL I have not been hypnotised.

ELIZABETH Really, Michael, you are jumping to conclusions.

MICHAEL I have not been hypnotised.

ELIZABETH I am not saying you have. I merely want to examine it as a possibility.

MICHAEL Bullshit. You can't hypnotise someone against their will.

ELIZABETH Quite so.

MICHAEL Then what the hell . . . ? You aren't saying I agreed.

ELIZABETH To what?

(MICHAEL *has no answer. He pours another drink.*)

ELIZABETH Let us just run through the events of this evening once again, shall we?

MICHAEL No, I'm not interested.

ELIZABETH You arrived at what time?

MICHAEL I said I'm not interested.

ELIZABETH Then I can't help you.

MICHAEL You know damn well what time I arrived.

ELIZABETH Are you sure?

MICHAEL I'm not even going to answer.

ELIZABETH What time do you think I think you arrived?

(*No response.*)

ELIZABETH Five past six?

MICHAEL Yes, for Christ's sake. Five past six.

ELIZABETH Quite right. And did you?

MICHAEL Yes.

ELIZABETH See. We got there in the end. You arrived at five past six. Then what?

MICHAEL All right, all right . . .

ELIZABETH You came straight here?

MICHAEL Yes.

ELIZABETH Along the High Street.

MICHAEL   Yes.

ELIZABETH Through the woods, over the gate. Up the garden path.

MICHAEL   I followed your map and instructions to the letter.

ELIZABETH How conscientious. Then what?

MICHAEL   I rang the bell. (*Points at dummy.*) She answered.

ELIZABETH Well wrapped up?

MICHAEL   I came in here. You seemed to be having trouble with your chair. I gave you a hand and you tricked me into thinking that I'd cut myself.

ELIZABETH And I helped patch you up?

MICHAEL   You seemed very kind.

ELIZABETH You didn't think it odd that I should have a first aid kit so readily to hand?

MICHAEL   I imagine you must have lots of things readily to hand.

ELIZABETH Did you think that then or are you just saying it now?

MICHAEL   It didn't seem odd, OK?

ELIZABETH Then what?

MICHAEL   We exchanged a few pleasantries. Then all this peculiar nonsense began.

ELIZABETH Did I offer you a drink?

MICHAEL   Yes.

ELIZABETH What did you have?

MICHAEL   I wanted water.

ELIZABETH   But?

MICHAEL   What is this?

ELIZABETH   You ended up having Coca Cola.

MICHAEL   Yes.

ELIZABETH   With brandy. When you refer to "peculiar nonsense" do you actually mean the scenes I had written?

MICHAEL   What do you think?

ELIZABETH   I think yes. And what was the first one?

MICHAEL   Jesus.

ELIZABETH   What was the first scene we enacted this evening?

MICHAEL   You know, Elizabeth. You know.

ELIZABETH   Yes, *I* do. But I want to be sure we're talking about the same thing.

MICHAEL   For Christ's sake.

ELIZABETH   I would be most grateful if you could recount it.

(*Pause.* MICHAEL *is torn.*)

MICHAEL   It was some perverted scene in which you probably wet your knickers while I kissed you.

ELIZABETH   It wasn't one you played having drunk a large brandy?

MICHAEL   No.

ELIZABETH   And it wasn't one in which I made a long speech in soothing tones which gradually made you feel more and more relaxed. Your eyelids didn't begin

ACT TWO

to feel heavy, you didn't begin to sink into that chair and fall into a long and deep trance?

MICHAEL   No!

ELIZABETH   And then I didn't hand you this script and ask you to memorise it?

MICHAEL   No.

ELIZABETH   And a couple of hours later, once you had completed the task – a terrific feat of memory I might add, but not unusual for subjects in a trance – I didn't tell you to forget about our first meeting? I didn't say, "We have never met. I want you to go back outside and when you come back in, we will play through, from memory, the script you have just read." And then I didn't click my fingers and wake you up?

MICHAEL   No.

ELIZABETH   I thought not.

MICHAEL   (*surprised*) What?

ELIZABETH   It is rather far fetched, isn't it?

MICHAEL   Jesus. Jesus.

ELIZABETH   Even for someone like you who is practised in memorising lines.

MICHAEL   Even if you'd . . .

ELIZABETH   What?

MICHAEL   Nothing.

ELIZABETH   No, what? Come on. Even if I'd what?

(*No response.*)

How good would you say you were at improvisation?

MICHAEL What the hell's that supposed to mean?

ELIZABETH It's what you are thinking, isn't it?

MICHAEL No.

ELIZABETH I should say you were very good. You could have filled in the gaps. Perhaps you're joining in with these games against your will. Yes. You might not even keep a diary. You're just temporarily under the illusion that you do. And maybe I didn't predict your actions earlier – you only thought I did, being in the state you are. Oh dear, Michael, you seem to be leading me to ideas I hadn't even thought of. Do you think it would be possible?

MICHAEL I know that I'm not hypnotised.

ELIZABETH I am glad you are so sure.

MICHAEL I'm positive.

ELIZABETH Good.

MICHAEL I don't need to prove it to anyone because I know.

ELIZABETH Well, that's fair enough.

MICHAEL If I was, I would know.

ELIZABETH Yes.

MICHAEL Wouldn't I?

ELIZABETH I should imagine so.

MICHAEL OK, I'm a bit drunk.

ELIZABETH I'll say.

MICHAEL But . . .

ELIZABETH   You are absolutely sure.

MICHAEL   Yes.

ELIZABETH   Just as a matter of interest, how long would you say you have been here?

(MICHAEL *looks at his watch*.)

ELIZABETH   Uh-uh, no cheating.

MICHAEL   You wound it forward.

ELIZABETH   How long, Michael?

MICHAEL   When you took my watch. You must have.

ELIZABETH   Must I? What I think you're trying to say is that you feel you have been here considerably less time than your watch indicates. And furthermore, that you are in complete control of yourself and that you have no doubt that you are your normal rational self.

MICHAEL   You're damn right.

ELIZABETH   How would you explain this peculiar nonsense?

(MICHAEL *stands up and pours a drink*.)

ELIZABETH   Do you seriously think that anyone in his right mind could really be persuaded that he had sustained a non-existent injury to his hand? Eh, Michael? Do you seriously think anyone in his right mind . . .

MICHAEL   Like you said, the blood, the . . .

ELIZABETH   "Suggestion of a mechanism"?

MICHAEL   Yes.

ELIZABETH   You don't know your own mind, do you? You can't trust your memory. You're not in control of your present. You're not sure of your own sanity. Why don't you tell me something about yourself? Who are you? Where do you come from? Where are you going? That sort of thing.

MICHAEL   I know who I am.

ELIZABETH   You think therefore you are.

(MICHAEL *emits a cynical snort.*)

ELIZABETH   Or: I think therefore you appear to be.

(MICHAEL *laughs. He goes over and looks at himself in the mirror.*)

MICHAEL   I don't need to prove anything because I know who I am.

ELIZABETH   But you need to look at your reflection.

MICHAEL   I make the reflection.

ELIZABETH   Your body makes the reflection.

(MICHAEL *continues staring at his reflection.*)

ELIZABETH   I wouldn't stare too long. If I were you. It can be most upsetting. It's like repeating the same word over and over. It loses its meaning. In the end it's just sound. All that is, Michael, is an arrangement of sensory receptors. It's not you it's just a face . . . a face . . . a face . . . a face . . .

(*But suddenly* MICHAEL *jerks his head away and she stops.*)

MICHAEL   I am an actor.

ELIZABETH   You are still clinging to that are you?

MICHAEL   I am an actor.

ELIZABETH You mean you are a man who stands in the dole queue on Tuesdays.

(MICHAEL *pours some more Scotch and gulps it down.*)

ELIZABETH Let me let you in on a secret. I told Estelle to tell you about the cupboard.

MICHAEL You're lying.

ELIZABETH I've been setting up traps for you all evening. And every time . . . so predictable.

(*He fumbles with his glass and it breaks. He looks at his hand. It is bleeding.*)

MICHAEL There. Look. That's real blood.

(*He wipes it on her face.*)

ELIZABETH Pain as a proof of consciousness – very interesting, Michael. Of course self-mutilation is one step towards madness. You're not an actor, Michael, you're a puppet. Acting requires some semblance of talent. You have no talent. You've been deluding yourself. You're a drunk. A talentless, alcoholic mother's boy.

(*He makes a fist and stands over her.*)

ELIZABETH I can make you do anything I want.

MICHAEL Then make me stop.

ELIZABETH Maybe I don't want you to.

(*He grabs her by the neck and squeezes.*)

MICHAEL I said stop me!

ELIZABETH (*spluttering*) I can't. I can't!

(*He stops. She slumps back in the chair, panting. They are both shaken.* MICHAEL *pours himself a drink.*)

MICHAEL I'm sorry.

(*He picks up the cloth and offers it to her.*)

ELIZABETH Get out.

MICHAEL It's still on your face. Please. I'm sorry.

ELIZABETH Go. Now.

(*He leaves the cloth on the arm of the chair. But he doesn't leave. She picks it up and wipes her face.*)

ELIZABETH Is that why they sacked you? Hot temper when drunk. Can't take criticism.

MICHAEL Look, I'm sorry. Sorry.

ELIZABETH And you expect me to apologise, too? Give me a drink.

(MICHAEL *pours her a Scotch and hands it to her. She takes a sip.*)

ELIZABETH You didn't know it at the time but it was your last but one performance. And my first. Afterwards I stood outside with all the other stage door johnnies – it's quite a club, as you probably know. In the old days, of course, I was on the other side. But I'm not proud. You get to recognise the faces, exchange stories, huddle together in the cold. One by one the cast came out and we got their autographs for the umpteenth time. Some of us had our photos taken. After half an hour all the soloists had left . . . except you. We waited and waited but gradually the group dispersed. Secretly I was quite pleased because I wanted you to myself. After an hour there were only three of us left. What were you doing all that time? No doubt you were enjoying the "rewards of success". Eventually you lurched out and my heart leapt even though you were with another woman. What was her name now . . . not Julia this time. Amy, I think it was. Anyway, there you were in the flesh. You were smaller than I'd imagined and less . . . striking, but nevertheless it was really you. I went up to you nervously and said – do you remember?

MICHAEL   No.

ELIZABETH I said, "Thank you for a wonderful performance, I thought you were terrific," and I held up my pen and the programme. And what did you do? Eh?

MICHAEL   I don't know. I can't remember. What did I do?

ELIZABETH You laughed in my face.

MICHAEL   I must have been drunk.

ELIZABETH You laughed in my face and you slouched off into the night with that floosie.

MICHAEL   I was drunk.

ELIZABETH And that's an excuse, is it? Well, we all looked at each other, the three of us, shocked, sheepish, humiliated. I'd already missed my train. I had to get a taxi. It was either that or stay in a hotel. Sixty miles, plus I had to pay over the odds because the driver said he wouldn't be able to get a return fare. After half an hour I began to doze off. I had to be up early to teach a class in the morning. I don't know how long I'd drifted off for but I was woken by the sound of a tremendous crack. At the time I thought it came from the roof but now I realise it must have been where the brick hit the windscreen – imagine that, a whole brick thrown up by the lorry in front. We swerved into the central reservation and rebounded backwards from the barrier into the fast lane. I remember, very clearly, the driver's head flipping back against the partition. I can see it now, his bald patch against the glass – funny, isn't it, what you remember? Next thing I knew I was on the floor, scrabbling around and screaming. Do you know what it's like to feel that helpless? We had almost stopped when the car behind smashed into the side of us. Now that, I don't remember. I don't remember the sound. And I didn't feel the pain. Not then. There comes a point when your body realises it has to give in. There was nothing I could do. Nothing. Nothing. The person you see sitting here is not me. I am active. I am co-ordinated. I am fit. I am agile. What you see is not me. I *am* no longer.

MICHAEL   I am sorry for what happened. It was tragic but it was an accident.

ELIZABETH   An accident?

MICHAEL   Yes! An accident – something beyond anyone's control. To blame me is madness.

ELIZABETH   There was a picture of you in the *Evening Standard* with your doting mother after your first night. (*She picks up the scrapbook.*) See? When asked how it felt to be an unknown thrust into the lead in a West End show you are quoted as saying, "I feel very lucky. I was disappointed not to get the part in the first place. But some things are meant to be." I wonder how poor Steven felt about that.

MICHAEL   I didn't mean that.

ELIZABETH   He was *meant* to have his overdose, was he?

MICHAEL   No.

ELIZABETH   So that you could get your chance? And if you were *meant* to get your chance then I was also *meant* to be crippled.

MICHAEL   No.

ELIZABETH   *No?*

MICHAEL   No.

ELIZABETH It wasn't *meant* to be?

MICHAEL   No.

ELIZABETH Then just think, Michael, how different the world would be for all of us if I had got that train. If only you'd come out a little earlier. If only you'd been able to get it up a little bit quicker. I liked your fantasy in your diary about the red button. A red button wired into your consciousness. Push it and you die. Painlessly. You don't really think you would have pushed it, do you? Even in your darkest hour? (*She pushes an imaginary button.*) Dead. Extinguished. Your whole life gone to waste. Pain is a useful deterrent.

           (ELIZABETH *opens the drawer of the desk and takes out the guns.*)

           Of course, these involve pain. When the bullets are real.

           (MICHAEL *is shocked and suddenly frightened. She loads a bullet into one of the guns and wheels over to cut off his route to the door.*)

ELIZABETH Or at least they probably do. Who knows? I imagine if you do it right, it doesn't hurt. Straight into the head. Through the brain. Too quick to be painful. (*She continues loading the bullets.*) You won't learn will you? I did warn you to leave. I urged you to. But you chose to stay.

MICHAEL   I didn't choose anything.

ELIZABETH You left but you came back. I ordered you to go. But you stayed all the same.

           (*She points the gun at him.*)

The more I go over the events of that evening, the more I try to make sense of them, the more I am sure that the responsibility is yours. You were the one who set it all in motion. Whichever way you look at it, the buck stops with you. So now, let's try to recall our dummy run. What did you say the options were? A run for the door? No? Then that leaves hiding or overpowering me. Well? What's it to be? Are we going to lock eyes? Are you going to psyche me out?

(MICHAEL *hesitates*. ELIZABETH *fires to miss and the window shatters.* MICHAEL *freezes momentarily and then hastily hides behind the armchair.*)

ELIZABETH   Oh, I see. Hiding. Fair enough.

MICHAEL   What are you going to do?

ELIZABETH   Oh, come on. I gave you all the signals. I planted all the signs. You helped me. Only a fool could fail to have seen them. You took away my freedom.

MICHAEL   Why me? Why not the person who left the brick in the road?

ELIZABETH   All I want is that you put me out of my misery.

MICHAEL   Or else?

ELIZABETH   Or else . . . I think you know what else.

MICHAEL   It's not fair.

ELIZABETH   Oh, I think it is.

MICHAEL   You chose to stay outside that stage door because you wanted to. I didn't ask you to. Perhaps you are right, it wasn't an accident. It wasn't an accident because deep down in your subconscious you wanted to miss your train. You wanted an excuse to enjoy the extravagance of a journey all the way home in a taxi. What an exciting story that would be to tell your drab little stage door friends. (*Mimics her voice.*) "I had to wait ages. Then I had to get a taxi all the way home. One hundred pounds. Can you believe it? Still he's going to be a star one day, mark my words."

ELIZABETH   No, Michael. All I wanted was an autograph and a safe journey home. I am intrigued that even in the face of death your vanity manages to get the better of you. I enjoyed your performance but nobody else did. I heard people sniggering at those high notes, shifting with embarrassment when you forgot your lines. Too tanked up to care. A star may have got away with it. But you were no star. Never were. Never will be. I was a victim. (*Suddenly screaming.*) Look at me! Look at me! You did this.

(*She wheels to try and get a better line on his legs. He moves out of sight. She aims at the dummy and fires. The dummy crashes over. She fires again, dangerously close, and the bullet impacts on the wall. Desperate,* MICHAEL *comes out from behind the armchair with his hands up.*)

MICHAEL   OK. OK. Please.

ELIZABETH   Ah, something different. What's this?

MICHAEL   Please don't shoot.

ELIZABETH   But I thought we agreed it was the only option.

MICHAEL   I'll do what you want.

ELIZABETH   You mean you'll pull the trigger? Because that's what I want.

(MICHAEL *drops his hands.*)

ELIZABETH   No, don't move a muscle. Michael, are you saying you'll pull the trigger without my wounding you first?

(*She points the gun at his legs.*)

MICHAEL   No . . . Yes.

ELIZABETH   But then how will you argue self-defence?

MICHAEL   I'll do it.

ELIZABETH   You know, I almost believe you. I think *you* almost believe you. But if I give you this gun without disabling you first, things change. You'll shoot me in the arm – we've been through all that.

MICHAEL   I won't. I won't.

ELIZABETH   It's a nice idea but . . .

(*She takes aim at his leg.*)

MICHAEL   No. Please!

ELIZABETH   All right. I'll tell you what – I'll think about it. We've got a bit of dialogue to do first.

MICHAEL   What?

ELIZABETH   Uh-uh, don't move. I swear to you Michael, the slightest hint of movement and I'll level the sides. So now, tell me, what is the purpose of punishment? Eh, Michael?

MICHAEL   I . . .

ELIZABETH   Revenge?

MICHAEL   What is this?

ELIZABETH   It's a conversation I want us to have. Well? Are you going to answer me? Would you agree that revenge is the purpose of punishment?

MICHAEL   Well yes, I suppose . . . partly.

ELIZABETH   What else?

MICHAEL   I don't know.

ELIZABETH   You don't know?

MICHAEL   No.

ELIZABETH   To deter, perhaps?

MICHAEL   Yes.

ELIZABETH   What else?

MICHAEL   Jesus.

ELIZABETH   Come on.

MICHAEL   I don't know.

ELIZABETH   Come on.

MICHAEL   What do you want me to say!?

ELIZABETH   I want you to say, "The main purpose of punishment is to re-empower the victim so that he can begin to feel better about himself." Well go on then.

(MICHAEL *gives a nervous laugh.*)

ELIZABETH   "The main purpose . . ."

MICHAEL   You're not serious.

(*She aims the gun.*)

MICHAEL   "The main purpose of punishment is to re-empower the victim . . ."

ELIZABETH   "So that he can begin to feel better about himself."

MICHAEL   "So that he can feel better about himself."

ELIZABETH   "Begin to."

MICHAEL   "The main purpose of punishment is to re-empower the victim so that he can begin to feel better about himself."

ELIZABETH Very good. You should be an actor. Do you understand it?

MICHAEL   Yes.

ELIZABETH Are you sure?

MICHAEL   I think so.

ELIZABETH You think you're sure?

MICHAEL   I am sure.

ELIZABETH Good. Now, I've thought about your suggestion and I'm willing to give it a go. After all, if I don't wound you, it'll be even more likely you'll get a jail sentence. How neat. How beautiful. My release from life leads to your incarceration for life.

MICHAEL   I'd explain. I'd get Estelle to testify. I'd show them your script.

ELIZABETH Michael. Really. You shouldn't be saying that. I might change my mind. So let's see. We're going to have to be very careful and move very slowly. If you make a sudden movement I'll fire. I swear it. Even if I suspect you *might* make a sudden movement, I'll fire. Then I'll put a bullet in the base of your spine for good measure. Of course I might end up having to shoot myself – but I can live with that. So to speak. Now move closer.

           (MICHAEL *steps slowly towards her.*)

ELIZABETH Slower.

           (*Keeping the gun in her right hand trained on him she picks up the other gun with her left hand and points the barrel at her forehead.*)

ELIZABETH Now lift your right hand.

(*He lifts his hand slowly to receive the butt of the gun. She is careful to make sure that the barrel is kept pointing straight between her eyes. He takes hold of it and she keeps hold of his arm with her left hand.*)

So here we are. The moment we've been destined for since you first set foot in this room. Oh, it's a wonderful feeling. I feel very calm. Very certain. You'll write that in your diary won't you? Goodbye, Michael. Five. Four. Three. Two. One.

(MICHAEL *closes his eyes and pulls the trigger. No bullet. No bang.* MICHAEL *opens his eyes and sees* ELIZABETH *smiling at him. He retches.*)

MICHAEL You bitch.

(*He retches again, dizzy with shock and humiliation.*)

ELIZABETH You know, you flatter yourself if you think I'm obsessed by *you*. Because I'm not. It's not you that interests me, it's what you stand for.

MICHAEL Shut up.

ELIZABETH And you know what that is, don't you, Michael?

MICHAEL You fucking bitch.

ELIZABETH But it's all nonsense isn't it – that stuff about destiny. Nothing is inevitable. Nothing is meant to be. When you actually do lose your freedom you really begin to understand that, don't you?

(*She lays the gun aside.*)

ELIZABETH No, only the weak believe in destiny. Nothing is written. Just because it's in the script doesn't mean it has to happen. You must take control of your life. Like I have. Else you're no more alive than that thing.

(*She points at the dummy.*)

ELIZABETH Don't be passive. Be active. Be strong.

(*She screws the lid back on the bottle of Scotch and takes it over to the drinks cabinet.*)

ELIZABETH And give up the drink. I mean really give it up. You're not programmed. It's not in your genes. That's just an easy excuse.

MICHAEL Shut up.

(*She takes the boxes over to the desk and tidies away the programmes and the scripts.*)

ELIZABETH Really, you could still make something of your life. You don't have to be anything you don't want to be. Look at me – it's never too late. It's quite a feeling, I must say, to be re-empowered. Quite a feeling. And a pretty good performance, eh? For an amateur. Mind you, you weren't bad yourself – a touch too cowardly for my taste, but not bad.

MICHAEL Shut up.

ELIZABETH Real bullets, yes, to make me look serious. But I'd never have fired. I don't want you to die. I'd never get away with it.

MICHAEL Shut up!

ELIZABETH If you'd only called my bluff, if you'd only had a little sense, a little courage, you could have . . .

(MICHAEL *snatches up her gun and points it at her.*)

MICHAEL Shut up, will you!

(ELIZABETH *freezes and then turns slowly to look at him.* MICHAEL *wrestles with himself, trying to fight off his anger and the impulse to pull the trigger.*)

ELIZABETH You don't think I'd have left it loaded.

(MICHAEL *checks the barrel. It is loaded.*)

ELIZABETH Come on, you don't want to.

MICHAEL I'm warning you!

ELIZABETH I did this for you. Don't you see – for both of us.

(MICHAEL *grips his right arm with his left, desperately trying to pull it off target.*)

ELIZABETH You can do it. You can control yourself. I'm sorry I made you angry. I really am.

MICHAEL (*imploring her*) Shut up.

ELIZABETH You see, I'm right, aren't I? You have the power.

(MICHAEL *seems to be pulling his arm off line.*)

MICHAEL Shut up.

ELIZABETH You have the power. You do.

(MICHAEL's *grip on the gun relaxes.*)

ELIZABETH (*arms open*) Come here. Come to me.

(*He takes a pace forward.*)

ELIZABETH Good boy.

(MICHAEL *fires. We hear a loud report and* ELIZABETH *is thrown backwards in her chair, dead. Her limp body slumps forward onto the control lever of the wheelchair and she is impelled towards* MICHAEL. *Paralysed, he watches in horror as she crashes into his legs, trapping him against the armchair. The lights come down.*)